MANHATTAN MAFIA GUIDE

Mulberry Street, 1900. *Detroit Publishing Company, Library of Congress.*

Mulberry Street today. *Courtesy of Shirley Dluginski.*

MANHATTAN MAFIA GUIDE

Hits, Homes & Headquarters

Eric Ferrara
Foreword by Arthur Nash

THE
History
PRESS

Published by The History Press
Charleston, SC 29403
www.historypress.net

First published 2011

Manufactured in the United States

ISBN 978.1.60949.306.6

Library of Congress Cataloging-in-Publication Data

Ferrara, Eric.
Manhattan Mafia guide : hits, homes and headquarters / Eric Ferrara.
p. cm.
Includes bibliographical references.
ISBN 978-1-60949-306-6
1. Mafia--New York (State)--New York--History. 2. Criminals--New York (State)--New
York--Biography. 3. Crime scenes--New York (State)--New York--Guidebooks. 4. Hiding
places--New York (State)--New York--Guidebooks. 5. New York State (N.Y.)--Guidebooks.
I. Title.
HV6452.N72M3445 2011
364.1'06097471--dc23
2011021478

CONTENTS

CONTENTS

II. SOCIAL CLUBS AND HANGOUTS

CONTENTS

III. GANGLAND HITS

CONTENTS

FOREWORD
USA OR BUST

T hat life is all gone now," I'm frequently reminded by motion-picture actor Butch "the Hat" Aquilino, recalling the rough-and-tumble schemes of mobs and men who once monopolized the five boroughs. "There's nothing left."

A native of Mott Street, Butch the Hat has been a fixture of New York City's Little Italy district long enough to remember Don Vito Genovese strolling its concrete sidewalks like a bloodthirsty pope, and even long enough to have run the occasional errand for an elderly Samuel Levine—nicknamed "Red" on account of henna-colored hair and a big round face full of freckles—who in decades past was an iron-fisted enforcer for the Brooklyn Combination and who, or so it's been committed to Judaica, refused to commit an act of homicide during Shabbat, *even if you paid him.*

As though it happened over breakfast, Butch the Hat remembers an inauspicious morning during the late 1950s when Red Levine strolled into Ratner's famous delicatessen on Delancey Street—a spot where he and his most senior crime associates had been dining for nearly half a century—and went completely unrecognized by the fresh-faced new employees who greeted him. Made to wait for service like a *schnorrer*, Levine felt slighted, and fueled by equal parts fury and frustration, he acted out. Gripping the closest serving tray, in one nimble movement he riddled the pastrami-scented airspace with three dozen freshly baked pastries, and until the day he died, he swore he'd never return. Already, it was a new day dawning, and Red Levine, like the assorted mutts with whom he once ran these same streets, wasn't going gently into night.

Butch the Hat is a world-class reminiscer. When little more than a teenager, he witnessed an underworld slaying that later figured prominently in Martin Scorsese's classic film *Mean Streets*. Today, the place where it happened is reimagined as a Chinese market, but the men's room where gunshots rang out is still there, calling Butch back to events that few but he can remember. In Hollywood's version, the bloody-shirted victim was portrayed by actor David Carradine, but Butch the Hat knew the true-life versions of both victim and killer—one a degenerate alcoholic and the other a deranged Mafia aspirant who was himself later eliminated, his body deposited in the trunk of a stolen car. Before that car trunk, though, home was an apartment across the hall from Butch the Hat. To say the shooter knew where to locate a potential eyewitness would be a gross understatement. Butch lived and breathed just one cup of sugar from catastrophe.

The incident rattled him; day and night, Butch the Hat worried he'd be hauled in by police detectives spotted swarming the crime scene and then nailed on a charge of guilt by association. Too often for his comfort, those cases had a clever way of sticking, and Butch the Hat began to sweat. He knew the killer's identity, and that was much more, very possibly, than he'd care to admit to police. Weighing it out, he sought the counsel of an elder statesman of the neighborhood, finding him in his usual spot on Mulberry Street, near the entrance of a social club known as the Alto Knights. There, Butch told his story while his uncle, Peter DeFeo, the Genovese crime family's official armorer, listened in silence.

"Did you do it?" DeFeo asked casually as his nephew concluded his monologue. The older man scanned the opposite sidewalk for familiar faces, occasionally nodding or waving. Butch admitted he hadn't.

"No? You didn't? Then let the ones who did it worry."

And that, as it were, was that. With a few carefully selected syllables, the case was closed, and Butch the Hat hardly spared it another thought. If the cops hauled him in for questioning, he had nothing to hide. So *why* be in hiding?

Afterward, Butch the Hat came to recognize the value of his uncle's advice, soliciting it more often, and while doing so, he couldn't help but be awed by the degree of reverence with which full-grown men would approach DeFeo—it rivaled the veneration of Saint Gennaro in the annual street *festa*, which DeFeo was rumored to control. But even then, in his youth, Butch knew the stories that had coined his uncle's reputation—how DeFeo went into hiding when a woman coveted by Vito Genovese was widowed, her husband strangled on a Greenwich Village rooftop; and how he fled once again, this time to a resort hotel in the Catskills, when an associate nicknamed "the Shadow" was shot dead on the floor of a Brooklyn pool hall. Thirty years later, Butch read in the *New York Times* that the hoodlum who had accused his uncle of the crime was towed from Jamaica Bay, his hands bound together and a block of concrete hardened around each leg. Butch knew all about the dice games, the shylocking and how DeFeo would use his brother-in-law's name, or even wear his clothes, to throw off investigators. And there were other stories, too—even less flattering ones—but this was Peter DeFeo's world, and the fact that he had stayed in it so long translated to mean one thing: he knew what it took to survive.

A couple of years before Joey Gallo was gunned down on Mulberry Street, however, something happened—something never fully explained to Butch the Hat. His uncle may have sensed a sea change coming, something in the air that made him uneasy about the future, because he abruptly whisked his family away from the neighborhood, sequestering them all in a luxury hi-rise along Park Avenue. And there they stayed, in some sense never to return.

Instead of following them to the Upper East Side, though, DeFeo stayed put, satisfied to carry on his daily routine until, predictably enough, he was nudged to the sidelines by ambitious underlings and permitted to "retire" into relative seclusion. But even then, Pete DeFeo kept the law guessing: for several years after his passing, rackets detectives of the New York City Police Department were still openly speculating about his criminal activities.

But that's all over now, and Butch the Hat is among the first to concede that men like DeFeo went out of fashion with the stingy-brim fedora, an institution Butch the Hat tries to single-handedly resuscitate, both in cinema and in life.

Or maybe those customs died in a symbolic blaze of gunfire, as Butch the Hat has suggested at times, alongside "Crazy" Joe Gallo, lying sprawled and bleeding in Hester Street, staring blindly skyward in terror, astonishment or a blending of both. During that pre-dawn shootout in Little Italy, when Gallo's birth and death so sleekly intersected, some of gangland's most sacred codes of conduct were shattered. Some say forever.

"Those days are gone," repeats Butch the Hat once again—as if to persuade himself as well. In private, Joey Gallo seemed to have known it, too.

"Do you remember Ali Baba's favorite saying?" Gallo asked wistfully in a letter to his younger brother, lamenting the loss of a trusted friend, bushwhacked by rivals while Gallo was stuck behind bars.

"One Hundred Fifty Million Thousand Dollars!"

If he'd been home, Crazy Joe wrote, they'd have been together—"Alive or not."

"Kid Blast," perhaps sensing his older brother's resignation, wrote back reassuringly. "Yussel," he penned, playfully adopting the Yiddish for Joseph. "Our name, which was always synonymous with honor, loyalty and manhood, if anything, has become an irrevocable fact. Remember, and be at ease to know that whatever your Machiavellian mind comes up with, we have the same parents."

Again it would be, he promised, like it was in the good old days.

Arthur Nash

ARTHUR NASH has worked as a crime beat reporter, and his photographic essay "New York City Gangland" (2010) was praised by Selwyn Raab as the "Eye-Catching Crown Jewel of Mafia History." Nash is a key contributor to the National Museum of Crime & Punishment in Washington, D.C., as well as the City of Las Vegas's Museum of Organized Crime & Law Enforcement, also known as "The MOB Museum." His image library has been sampled by the Discovery, History and Biography Channels. He currently resides at the landmark Hotel Chelsea.

PREFACE

The very first thing you should know before embarking on a career in criminal research (or referencing any Mafia book, including this one) is that criminals lie—a lot. The second thing you should know is that journalists and authorities also embellish on occasion. (They can't all be the "biggest bust in history.") And the information we get from insiders—former Mafioso (rats), law enforcement officials and mob family members—is often skewed to fit a personal narrative. This means that many of the original source "facts" about *l'onorata società* that we have to work with are distorted to begin with. Outlined in this book are many examples of how trumped-up news reports, speculation and folklore have led to many inaccurate beliefs about the Mafia.

Some fantastic authors and researchers of late, like Selwyn Raab, Mike Dash, David Critchley, Arthur Nash and a handful of others, have shed unique light on the subject through personal insight, academic research and/or common sense—a far cry from the sensational Jimmy Breslin articles I grew up with—yet much of the information that is readily available to general audiences via insincere cable television shows, Hollywood movies, amateur blogging and cut-and-paste journalism remains carelessly unreliable.

Presented here is a directory of notable Mafia members who lived and operated in Manhattan over the last century, along with their known and reported home and business addresses, hangouts and so on, based on six years of active research and over a century of community insight. The sources for many of these addresses and stories are news reports, police records, government files, criminal biographies and personal accounts. I did my very best to cross-reference as much as possible by combing through thousands of original source documents and consulting with fellow authors, historians, mob family members, law enforcement officials and local elders to provide as accurate a representation of the subject matter as possible. However, the truth is that there may be many truths, and nobody knows anything *for sure*. (I tend not to trust anyone who claims otherwise.)

In no way is this book intended to glorify the Mafia or present Italians in a bad light. To be perfectly clear, 99.9 percent of Italians are, of course, noncriminals. That should go without saying. When I provide lectures or tours on the subject, I always start out by asking, "Can anybody name three people of Sicilian ancestry who are *not* criminals?" Many are surprised to learn that people like Tony Atlas, Joe DiMaggio, Supreme Court assistant justice Antonin Scalia, Frank Zappa, Cindy Lauper, jazz guitarist Pat Martino and many, many others who have positively contributed to our culture also happen to be of Sicilian heritage.

In New York City, Italians (they were all simply "Italians" once they arrived in America) played an invaluable role in the development of our

Illustration showing the sentiment toward Italian immigrants at the turn of the century. The lower left-hand panel shows Italians being drowned, with the caption, "The way to dispose of them." *The* Mascot, *September 7, 1899.*

16

infrastructure and the success of the city's booming garment and shipping industries. One hundred years ago, Italians dug the subway tunnels, swept the streets, unloaded cargo ships, sewed the clothing most Americans were wearing and built the structures many of us are living in now, literally brick by brick. Italians introduced native delicacies, arts, opera and theatrical works that would earn the adoration of the American public. They were successful in banking, sports and politics; established pioneering publishing ventures; became active in trade unions; organized social and political clubs; and opened businesses just like everyone else attempting to achieve the American dream.

When the gates of *L'Isola dell Lagrime* (Ellis Island, referred to as the "Island of Tears") opened in 1892, Italian immigrants poured into New York City. By 1900, almost a quarter of a million lived here, and two decidedly Italian districts emerged on opposite sides of Manhattan Island. Uptown, East Harlem sheltered a sizable Italian population; downtown, Italians divvied up what would become the largest population of Italians in the country.

Sadly, one of the biggest threats to the progress of Italians of the day came from other Italians. Many who arrived in the United States carried Old World prejudices toward other regional countrymen—and though most were not criminals, many obeyed the code of *omerta*, or "manhood," meaning you took care of your own business outside the law, which was either ineffectual or nonexistent back in the old country.

On a local level, a young man navigating the streets became a risky proposition, as walking a block or two in either direction from his home could earn him a couple of lumps on the ol' noggin or worse. For example, the Lower Manhattan Italian district, "Little Italy," at one time encompassed a vast portion of city real estate, the heart of which was between Worth and Houston Streets and Bowery and Sixth Avenue.

This district was actually divided into several micro neighborhoods. As a general rule, southern Italians settled west of Mulberry Street, and Sicilians to the east. Then those districts were divvied up even further. For example: the neighborhood between Delancey and East Houston Streets became home to immigrants from northern Sicily, in particular the province of Palermo. Each district had very distinct cultures, customs and even languages, yet to outsiders, it was all simply Little Italy.

The insulation and division among the population allowed localized protection rackets to thrive. Many citizens had initially accepted or tolerated this practice, as it had been part of life for generations back in Europe. No one was really immune. There was barely an "honor among thieves," let alone any moral codes regarding innocents, police or family members of enemies. The infamous Mafia code of "we only kill each other" was not established until much later. Everyone was subject to extortion, kidnapping and targeted and random violence and coercion. Bystanders were of no concern for gangland self-preservationists, and many innocents fell victim to petty underworld disputes.

One of the earliest threats to Italian immigrants in America was *La Mano Negra*, or the "Black Hand," which was simply an extortion tactic believed to have originated in seventeenth- or eighteenth-century Spain. It was adopted by southern Italians and transferred to America by the end of the nineteenth century.

GIUSEPPE DI PRIMO

Black Hand illustration. Oelwein *[Iowa]* Daily Register, *June 7, 1909.*

"Black Hand Terror" illustration, September 16, 1909. Black & White, *March 19, 1910.*
Drawn by Will Owen.

Black Hand criminal networks were well established in New York City by
the turn of the century. It was perhaps the most rudimentary and transparent
form of extortion possible, as simple as sending someone a threatening note
requesting a certain amount of money by a specific date. The note was
usually signed with a drawing of a black hand (hence the name) or another
ominous symbol, like a noose, dagger or skull.

As a businessman, once you received that note, there was very little you
could do. If you did not meet the demands of the request, then almost
certain harm would come to you or your business by way of arson, assault,
kidnapping or even murder. One retaliatory method of choice for many
black handers in New York City at the time was bombing—if you did not or
could not pay, the extortionist might simply blow up your store.

Bombings were not isolated incidents by any means. In 1907, fifty-two
bombings in Manhattan's Italian communities were attributed to the Black
Hand.[1] That is an average of one storefront blown to bits a week. Remember,
these were tightly packed residential neighborhoods; casualties were of no
concern. The more successful you were, the larger a target you became. For
example, one of the most famous Italians in America at the time, star tenor
Enrico Caruso, was famously black handed for $15,000.

Fast forward a generation and the Italian underworld began to take on
a different image. First-generation Americans and those who arrived at an

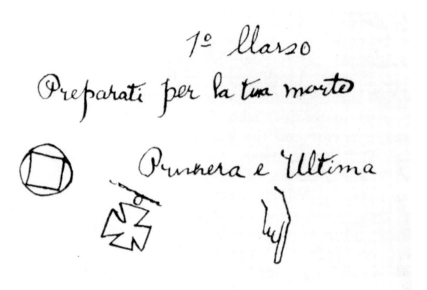

Black Hand note: "Prepare for your death. Last & Final." State Center Enterprise [Iowa].

Outside Pati's Bank, 238–40 Elizabeth Street, 1908. This photo was taken two months after a Black Hand bomb wrecked the counter on January 23, 1908. Five bombs were exploded on this single block over the course of that year. *Library of Congress.*

early age began to outnumber the traditionalist, right-off-the-boat patriarchs who controlled *La Cosa Nostra* for the first few decades. Those bred in the United States did not carry the same kind of prejudices toward non-Italians, nor did they care about Old World provincial rivalries among their own kind. By the end of Prohibition, what started as a "way of life" turned into a business, and like any business, public image was key to success.

Charlie Luciano allegedly once said, "Arnold Rothstein taught me how to dress." Gangsters discovered that a little class, tact and intelligence could get them further than pure street thuggery. By the early 1930s, rules had been established within the Mafia that curbed violence between members and outsiders. You couldn't really just murder someone, move in on their territory or create your own rackets anymore—without permission. The days of shaking down neighborhood merchants for a few dollars were dwindling as gangsters focused their efforts on much more lucrative ventures, like narcotics, for example. A lot of die-hards do not want to admit it to this day, but drug trafficking made the Mafia possibly hundreds of millions of dollars between the 1930s and 1950s. Unless there was a truly massive conspiracy involving hundreds of international agencies and police departments spanning several decades, the records are pretty hard to dispute. Though most families swore off the *junk* by the end of the 1950s, a few renegades continued for a while after. The stories of Mafia members being killed or excommunicated for dealing or using drugs behind the backs of their bosses are probably accurate. It was too risky a business to be associated with.

There was an enormous difference between the Mafia of 1905 and the Mafia of 1935. Luciano stayed at the poshest hotels and drove the most expensive cars—a far cry from the man who founded the family that "Lucky" inherited, Giuseppe Morello, who slept in a filthy, cramped, one-room attic on Christie Street.

The public's fascination with the Mafia dates back to at least the post-Prohibition era of the early 1930s when Al Capone was being hounded by paparazzi and George Raft was thrilling audiences on the big screen with his infectious swagger. The gangster—bank robbers, bandits and rumrunners who lived fast and rebelled against the system—had become a folk hero to many. But really, very little was known at the time about the inner workings of a Mafia crime family or their history. Even the U.S. government, as uncovered through released internal memos, was not fully privy to secrets of the *Fratelanza*.

In an age where Vito Corleone and Tony Soprano are household names in even the farthest reaches of the planet, it is hard to imagine what the public's perception of the Mafia was before October 1, 1963. That is the day Genovese family button man turned informer Joseph Valachi took the stand on national television and introduced the idea of La Cosa Nostra to the masses. Americans were glued to their television sets as the former street soldier told his version of Mafia history. It was one of the highest-rated programs that CBS had ever run and was called "exciting and frightening to watch."[2]

About the same time American Mafia turncoat Valachi was spinning his tale, a Sicilian Mafioso named Nicola Gentile spilled his guts with the 1963 book *Vita Di Capo Mafia*. Joe Valachi released his memoirs soon after, and another high-profile informer turned up in 1968 under the name "Jim Carra" (see Attardi, Alphonso).

By the time Jim Carra publicly corroborated the testimony of Valachi and Gentile, the public was still sorting out the assassination of John Kennedy, and the United States was neck deep in the Vietnam War. With speculation of secret societies and conspiracies abounding, the Mafia and pop culture were about to collide like never before.

Mario Puzzo's *The Godfather* hit the shelves in March 1969, and just three years later (in March 1972), Francis Ford Coppola transformed it into the iconic motion picture. Also in 1972, *The Valachi Papers* was turned into a movie starring Charles Bronson, and *The Last Testament of Lucky Luciano*, allegedly written from the memoirs of the vice kingpin, made a huge splash in 1974 (see Luciano, Charlie).

In real life, the Colombos were at war with themselves, and the Bonannos were at war with almost everyone; the Racketeer Influenced and Corrupt Organizations (RICO) Act was established in 1970; Jimmy Hoffa disappeared in 1975; and the Mafia was making headlines on a daily basis. The public was hooked (from the safety of their living rooms). According to the Internet Movie Database (IMDB), on a list of the "Top 100 Movies of All Time," the top two are *The Godfather* (#2) and *The Godfather II* (#1).

I have no personal connection to any of the subjects, but like many working-class, multigenerational New Yorkers over a certain age with Italian blood, I became a little familiar with the culture of La Cosa Nostra; it was practically unavoidable for many years in this city. There was a social club (or three) on almost every block in certain neighborhoods. They ran the street festivals and organized block parties. We went to church and school (or played hooky) with members' sons and daughters, and their parents attended PTA meetings and Little League games like everyone else. One neighbor was a cop, one was a truck driver and one was a wise guy.

It was not uncommon to see the ailing Genovese boss, Frank "Funzi" Tieri, at the boccie ball courts in Brooklyn in the 1970s. Like many other Italian grandfathers of the day, he was always armed—with pockets full of hard candy for the kids. Vincent Gigante could regularly be seen walking home with a plastic shopping bag full of tomatoes that he grew at a local community garden on the Lower East Side, sharing his surplus with neighbors along the way. Mafioso blended into society in much the same way as the butcher, baker and candlestick maker.

That was "Old New York." The days of blue-collar, ethnic-based neighborhoods are fading, and the "members only" clubs—once unmistakable—are long gone. As I always say in jest, where the rest of the world uses BC and AD to measure time, here in New York City we have "Before Giuliani" and "After Giuliani."

It is a different city now. For better or for worse, the Mafia's presence is virtually nonexistent. As presented in the "Social Clubs and Hangouts" chapter of this book, decades-old mob cafés have been transformed into Chinese wholesalers, chichi boutiques and trendy eateries. Most multigenerational Italian families have been uprooted from Manhattan since the 1970s. Natives now jokingly refer to the old neighborhood, which has been relegated to about two city blocks, as "*Very* Little Italy."

This book was written in the hope that the reader has a basic understanding of the subject matter and is familiar with terms like "Mafia Commission" or "Five Families." If you need a primer, I highly suggest starting off with David Critchley's *The Origin of Organized Crime in America: The New York City Mafia, 1891–1931* and Selwyn Raab's *Five Families: The Rise, Decline, and Resurgence of America's Most Powerful Mafia Empires*. And be sure to pick up a copy of Arthur Nash's *New York City Gangland*, which is chock full of unique, insightful stories and rare images you won't find anywhere else.

I
PROFILES

ATTARDI, ALPHONSO

499 East Eleventh Street, 14 East Twenty-third Street
Alias: Altroad DeJohn, Jim Carra[?]
Born: 1897,[3] Porto Empedocle, Sicily
Died: 1972, Suffolk County, New York
Association: D'Aquila, Mangano/Gambino crime families

Many of those in the know believe this five-foot, four-inch, 160-pound veteran mobster turned informant was the same person who shared his life story with veteran journalist Jack Anderson in the late 1960s under the name Jim Carra.

In a widely redistributed January 28, 1968 article published by *Parade Magazine*, entitled "A Top Killer Spills Mob Secrets," a former mobster with a curiously similar background to Attardi's provided intimate details of everything from the protocols of a Mafia initiation ceremony to the murder of Albert Anastasia.

Unlike Joe Valachi, whose testimony offered a wealth of information but yielded few arrests, the information Attardi provided to authorities in the 1950s led to a massive infiltration of organized crime that resulted in several convictions. Also unlike Valachi, who has become a household name to even the most casual mob enthusiast, very little has been written about (or even reported on) Attardi.

Let's start with what we do know from released government files and the few news reports available on the elusive gangster. In 1922, Attardi served a four-month sentence for the violation of the Harrison Act, which was passed in 1914 "to impose a special tax on all persons who produce, import, manufacture, compound, deal in, dispense, sell, distribute, or give away opium or coca leaves, their salts, derivatives, or preparations."

A January 15, 1947 internal memo from the Federal Bureau of Narcotics (FBN) field office in New York City claimed that Attardi admitted to attending a 1937 meeting on the outskirts of Houston, Texas, on the farm of Don Vincenzo Vallone. (To whom he admitted this detail is recorded as "unknown.") In attendance, according to the report, was Dallas mob boss Joseph T. Piranio and underboss Joseph F. Civello.

The reason for the meeting is unknown, though we do know that on October 5, 1937, Attardi; his wife, Josephine "Jose" Attardi, alias "G. Altroad"; and fourteen others were swept up in a coordinated interstate roundup, suspected of conspiring to import narcotics from Europe and distribute them through New York, Texas and Louisiana.

Alphonso Attardi was held in the Galveston County (Texas) Jail until posting $10,000 bond on December 14, 1937. On January 31, 1938, he and his wife were extradited back to New York City, where sixteen of the eighty-eight people named in the indictment were brought to trial in May 1938. Several opted to plead guilty in lieu of facing a jury. At least two witnesses testified to delivering drugs for Attardi from a Galveston nightclub called Turf. On June 2, 1938, Alphonso Attardi was sentenced to two years in Leavenworth, plus a $5,000 fine.[1] His wife received two years plus a $1,000 fine, though that was later reduced to five years' probation.

On May 9, 1950, the FBN headquarters in Washington, D.C., furnished a list of twenty-four Mafia suspects operating in Texas. Among the names on record were New York Mafioso Vito Genovese and Vincent Rao; Attardi was listed as operating in Houston.

Other than that, only two authors that I know of have mentioned Attardi. According to 1963's *Border Guard: The Story of the United States Customs Service* by Don Whitehead, Attardi spent eight years in the 1940s behind bars on narcotics violations and faced deportation to Italy upon release.

The author goes on to say that Attardi fell in love with a twenty-two-year-old waitress and feared deportation, so he offered himself up to federal authorities. By 1952, Attardi was working with the FBN to set up several successful undercover sting operations, for which he received a paltry $5,000 and disappeared with his new lover.

In *The Great Pictorial History of World Crime* (volume one, published in 2004), author Jay Robert Nash adds that Attardi's 1940s conviction was a "bum rap" and that while he was in prison, Attardi's wife passed away and he lost his oil and cheese importing store on Chrystie Street.[5]

Beyond that, the trail pretty much dries up for Alphonso Attardi. If we are to believe the 1968 claims of Jim Carra, who was admittedly speaking in anonymity under an assumed name, the gangster was initiated into a Sicilian Mafia organization as a teenager before immigrating to New York City in 1919. Here, he started as a bootlegger working for the D'Aquila crime family in the 1920s and went on to watch the Mafia evolve in its most formative years.

"The honor, respect and morality that had been instilled into me in Sicily all became secondary matters. The big thing in the United States was money and more money," Carra recalled, disenchanted with the greed that polarized the Italian underworld during Prohibition.

BIONDO, JOSEPH

245 East Twenty-first Street, Manhattan, 1930

Alias: Joe Bandy, Joe the Blonde

Born: April 16, 1897, Barcellona Pozzo di Gotto, Sicily (b. Biondi, Giuseppe)

Died: June 10, 1966, New York City

Association: D'Aquila family, Gambino crime family underboss

Biondo was a veteran gangster of the bootlegging wars with an influential criminal career spanning four decades. It is believed that Biondo was involved in the plot to kill both Salvatore Maranzano in 1931 and Albert Anastasia in 1957. He was a perpetual member of Interpol's International List of Narcotics Violators[6] and alleged overseer of the Mangano/Anastasia family drug-trafficking operations throughout the early 1950s.

Around the East Village—the neighborhood where Biondo spent much of his life after emigrating from Italy as a baby in 1898—he was mostly known as "Bandy," but with a thick Lower East Side accent, it came out almost as "bain-tee." Some insiders from the old neighborhood had no idea it was spelled with a "D" until seeing it in print later on.

The five-foot-four, 150-pound gangster wielded great influence over younger neighborhood toughs and befriended early on future top-level Mafioso like Charlie Luciano, who claimed to have pickpocketed immigrants while living with Biondo on Fourteenth Street as a kid. The two would be close for the rest of their lives.

On July 4, 1931, Biondo, Luciano and Tommy Lucchese were apprehended together in a Cleveland hotel room and questioned during a police investigation; however, no charges were filed. They were in Ohio to watch Max Schmeling defend the heavyweight title against W.L. Stribling. (Schmeling won by KO in the fifteenth round).

One theory suggests that sometime in 1931, Biondo was visited by Frank Scalise, the newly installed boss of what would become the Gambino crime family. *Capo di tuti capi* Salvatore Maranzano awarded Scalise the position after the Castellammarese War of 1930–31, allegedly with the stipulation that he must help kill another family boss named Vincent Mangano. Scalise couldn't go through with the murder and went to Biondo about the plan. Biondo then alerted Mangano, Luciano and others. Maranzano was dead by the end of the year.

In the spring of 1942, Biondo quite openly visited exiled Charlie Luciano in Italy and, as expected, was picked up by authorities in Milano and questioned. Biondo insisted he was in Italy for legitimate business on behalf of major corporations back in the States; however, these companies denied knowing Biondo. No evidence could be found of wrongdoing at the time, but it is believed that Luciano introduced Biondo to a third-party supplier of acetic acid, used to cut heroin for street sale. Biondo made several trips to see Luciano over the years, some believe to deliver Luciano his financial share of various rackets going on back in North America.

In October 1958, the FBN intercepted a letter intended for Biondo from fellow Mafioso Nicola Gentile that read, in part, "The road you have taken by virtue of your intelligence has brought you to a superior social level so that today you are a LEADER and well regarded."[7]

Undercover authorities then posed as representatives of Biondo and met with Gentile, fooling him into providing delicate information. When the narcotics agents unveiled their true identities, Gentile decided to testify against the Mafia.

Joe Valachi claimed that Biondi was involved with Carlo Gambino in the 1957 murder of Albert Anastasia, which earned the capo a spot as underboss to Gambino (who replaced Anastasia as head of the family). He also claimed that Biondo was a member of the Mafia Commission.

An internal FBI memo dated October 3, 1967, states that a source claimed Biondo fell out of favor with Carlo Gambino for his chronic participation in narcotics trafficking and even went so far as to say that Gambino ordered a hit on Biondo by the end of 1965. By that time, Biondo was spending much of his time with his New York City–born wife, Louise Volpe (whom he married in 1925), at their second home at 1936 South Ocean Drive in Hallandale, near Miami Beach, Florida.

Joseph Biondo died in 1966 and was succeeded as underboss of the Gambino family by Aniello Dellacroce. His brother, John Joseph Biondo, was an alleged soldier in the Gambino family at the time of Joseph's death.

BUIA, ANGELO ANTHONY

719 Lexington Avenue, 1950s
Alias: Frenchie, Angelo Russo
Born: July 26, 1910, Nice, France
Died: May 3, 2003, Montgomery, Maryland
Association: Genovese crime family

French-born to Sicilian parents, Angelo Anthony Buia and his brother, Matildo, were considered by the FBN to be major heroin distributors for the Accardi-Campisi crew of the Genovese family.

In August 1955, Buia pleaded guilty to possession of thirty-five ounces of heroin. When a previous conviction for narcotics violations was disclosed, he was sentenced to seven years in prison as a second offender.[8]

In August 1962, Buia and five other mobsters, including Benedetto Cinquegrana and Carmine Locascio, pleaded not guilty to charges of operating an international drug ring suspected of smuggling over $100 million worth of heroin into the United States over a ten-year period.[9] Authorities believed Buia obtained massive amounts of heroin from French sources for three of five Mafia families in New York.[10]

In December 1963, eleven of sixteen indicted New York mobsters were sentenced to seven to twenty-five years in prison; however, all charges were reversed in August 1964 by an appeals court judge.

BUIA, MATILDO

203 Prince Street, Manhattan, 1950s
Alias: Ralph Stella
Born: October 18, 1907, Castellammare, Sicily
Died: November 23, 1988, New York City
Association: Genovese crime family

Along with his brother Angelo, Matildo was suspected of being involved in international narcotics trafficking for over two decades during the mid-twentieth century.

Matildo's first arrest on narcotics violations came in 1933, with another conviction in 1938. On August 3, 1955, Matildo and Angelo Buia were arrested for trying to sell approximately thirty-five ounces of heroin to undercover narcotics agents. Matildo was sentenced to five years in prison[11] and was released under probation on April 5, 1959.

CATALDO, JOSEPH

125 Sullivan Street, 1920, 1930; 59 West Twelfth Street, 1950s
Alias: Joe the Wop
Born: November 16, 1908, Basilicata, Italy (b. Cataldo, Giuseppe)
Died: July 1980, New York City
Association: Most prominent twentieth-century mobsters

Perhaps most infamous for his alleged ties to Lee Harvey Oswald assassin Jack Ruby, Cataldo was a major twentieth-century mobster, racketeer, loan shark, casino manager, nightclub owner and entertainment industry mover and shaker.

Eight-year-old Cataldo arrived in New York City with his family on November 27, 1916, on the steamship *Duca d'Aosta* and earned his status as a U.S. citizen in September 1933. Not much is recorded about his initiation into organized crime or his early career with the mob, though it has been implied that his foray into crime began during Prohibition.

According to the Wop himself, he managed a Havana, Cuba casino "in the good old days."[12] By the end of the 1950s, Cataldo operated several wildly popular and successful nightclubs and restaurants in New York City, like Chandler's, the Camelot Supper Club and Tony Pastor's. (He is also said

125 Sullivan Street today. *Courtesy of Sachiko Akama.*

to have been tied to the famous jazz club Birdland.)[13] The Camelot became the unofficial headquarters for powerful star-broker George Wood of the William Morris Agency, the man responsible for the careers of superstars like Frank Sinatra.[14] In 1962, George Wood and Joseph Cataldo partnered in a downtown Vegas casino called Pioneer Club.[15]

Cataldo gained some national notoriety in 1963 when the FBI traced back to him a phone call thought to have been placed by Jack Ruby on July 7 of that year, just four months before the murder of Oswald. When questioned on December 11, 1963, Cataldo denied knowing Ruby, but an informant told the FBI that Ruby booked "talent"—all of whom turned out to be gangsters—for his Dallas nightclub through Cataldo.

In August 1968, Cataldo and five others were indicted for stock fraud,[16] and in February 1980, he was accused of being involved in a plot to disrupt what was known as the "Black Tuna" trial by paying off federal witnesses and assassinating a district court judge. Cataldo died of a heart attack during the trial.

CINQUEGRANA, BENEDETTO

*122 Mott Street, 1920; 209 Grand Street, 1930s;
166 Mulberry Street, 1950s*

*Alias: Benedetto DiPalo, Vincent Grande, ChinkBorn: January 6, 1913,
New York City*

Died: August 17, 2002, Englewood Cliffs, New Jersey

Association: Genovese crime family

Cinquegrana grew up in the heart of Little Italy, where his butcher father, Luigi, operated a meat market at 156 Mott Street. His parents were married in 1908 in Cesa, Italy (mother Concetta's hometown), and immigrated to New York City in 1910 with their eldest son, Francesco. Here, they settled at 122 Mott Street, where Benedetto was born in 1913. The future gangster would spend most of his life in his native neighborhood and held interest in several local businesses, like the mob hangout Caffe Roma on Broome Street, where he was listed as vice-president of the corporation. (Fellow wise guy Eli Zeccardi, a future Genovese underboss, was president.)

122 Mott Street, the childhood home of Benedetto Cinquegrana, today. *Courtesy of Shirley Dluginski.*

Convicted of armed robbery by the time he was sixteen years old, Cinquegrana racked up a few arrests for bookmaking in the 1930s and 1940s before turning his attention to narcotics in the 1950s.

Cinquegrana may have earned one of his nicknames because of his associations with Chinese drug smugglers, like Wong Gum Hoy, with whom he was arrested on February 17, 1956, after feds seized from them a half pound of opium.[17] In 1962, forty-nine-year-old Benedetto Cinquegrana was one of several men (including Angelo Buia) arraigned as members of an international narcotics ring that was suspected of trafficking tens of millions of dollars' worth of pure heroin into the country over a nine-year period.[18] Charges were dismissed after appeal.

On December 13, 1972, Cinquegrana was called to testify before the Waterfront Commission during an investigation into possible mob racketeering at a Port Elizabeth stevedore company; he pleaded the Fifth and refused to answer any questions.

On December 15, 1981, Cinquegrana did plead guilty to "conspiracy to commit offense or to defraud the United States" and was sentenced to a five-year suspended sentence.[19]

His last known address was 57 Sherwood Avenue in Englewood Cliffs, New Jersey, where he passed away in August 2002 at eighty-nine years old.

CIRAULO, VINCENZO JAMES

88 Second Avenue, Manhattan, 1950s

Alias: Jimmy Second Avenue, Jimmy Ninety-two, Jimmy East, Jimmy Fischetti

Born: September 8, 1919, New York City

Died: September 26, 1997, Palm Beach, Florida

Association: Lucchese crime family

The FBN identified Ciraulo as a "trusted and important member" of a Lucchese crew headed by Carmine Locascio. He operated the Stage Bar on East Fourth Street in the 1950s while living at 88 Second Avenue.

By the 1970s, Ciraulo was a respected Mafia veteran on the lam from New York authorities for outstanding loan-sharking warrants. While a fugitive in

Florida, he used the name Jimmy Fischetti and worked closely with Tampa mob boss Santo Trafficante Jr. Ciraulo's luck ran out when he was arrested by FBI agents on a holiday visit to New York City on January 22, 1980.[20] This arrest caused a small rift between the New York and Florida FBI offices, since Ciraulo was at the center of a long sting operation called Coldwater, in which undercover feds established a gambling casino called King's Court in Pasco County, Florida.

In the summer of 1986, sixty-eight-year-old Ciraulo pleaded guilty to conspiracy and extortion in connection with the Coldwater operation and was sentenced to two years in prison. His codefendant, Santo Trafficante, refused a plea deal and died during a lengthy trial just hours after receiving open heart surgery on March 17, 1987.

Ciraulo died at age seventy-eight while living in Royal Palm Beach, Florida. His funeral was held in the Bronx.

COSTELLO, FRANK

115 Central Park West, Apartment 18F, 1950s
Born: January 26, 1891, Calabria, Italy (b. Castiglia, Francesco)
Died: February 18, 1973, New York City
Association: Luciano/Genovese crime family

Frank Costello was one of the most successful gangsters in U.S. history and partial inspiration behind Marlon Brando's role in *The Godfather*. This crime kingpin lived in a luxury building at 115 Central Park West when, on May 2, 1957, he was shot in its lobby by Vincent "Chin" Gigante. He survived but got the message sent by Gigante's boss, Vito Genovese: it was time to retire.

Born in a small Calabrian village, the young Costello immigrated to New York City in 1900 at about nine years old. He arrived with his mother and older brother, to join their father, Luigi, who had established himself as a small grocery store proprietor in East Harlem before sending for the family back in Italy.

The future criminal icon skipped school and got into trouble early, racking up a slew of petty charges as a youth. He worked for the Morello-Terranova

Mug shot of a young Frank Costello.

gang in Harlem and made friends with other rising street thugs across the city as teen. By the time Prohibition hit, Frank Costello had made a name for himself in certain circles of the underworld and joined forces with Charlie Luciano, Vito Genovese, Meyer Lansky, Benjamin Siegel and others running booze locally in an operation funded by Arnold Rothstein.

In 1929, he played an important role in establishing the National Crime Syndicate, and during the Mafia restructuring of 1931, Costello earned the consigliere position in the new Luciano crime family, making him third in command behind Luciano and underboss Vito Genovese. Costello proved to be one of the most business-minded gangsters of the era, and he made the Luciano family a fortune in the slot machine, race wire, loan-sharking and casino rackets.

By 1937, with boss Luciano behind bars and underboss Genovese in Italy evading murder charges, Costello became acting boss of the family. Under his direction, the organization acquired a near monopoly on various gambling enterprises across the United States. He had become so wealthy and powerful that virtually every crooked politician and city administrator of the era was either installed by Costello or in his pocket.

Costello was said to be one of the last of the old-timers who did not promote the sale of narcotics; he felt it was not worth the risk. Too many low-level criminals and associates outside the family had to be involved, and potentially long prison sentences made people talk. In what would be proven by the 1950s, a single street pusher turned informant had the potential to put an entire crew behind bars.

If it weren't for murder, graft, extortion and otherwise illegal practices, Costello would have been remembered as one of the most prominent and ingenious businessmen of the era, and he wanted to be respected as such. Costello worked hard to maintain a clean image; his social circle included the highest-level politicos, entertainers, industrialists and socialites of the generation.

Well liked and highly respected, the crime lord's only real threat came from inside his own family. When Vito Genovese returned to America, he believed the boss position was his, only found that it was extremely difficult to gather any support for an overthrow. Costello simply made everyone too much money and had too many powerful allies.

Genovese was the opposite of Costello. He was said to be brutish and violent and had made many enemies in his career. He did allegedly promote narcotics trafficking and had none of the business or social savvy that made Frank Costello so successful. It didn't appear that Costello had anything to worry about; however, things started to unravel for him in the early 1950s.

Luciano family underboss Guarino "Willie" Moretti—Costello's blood cousin and most trusted associate—was murdered in a Clifton Park, New Jersey diner on October 4, 1951. It was a major personal and professional setback for Costello.

Then, in 1952, he served his first prison term in over thirty years: eighteen months for refusing to answer questions during the infamous Kefauver hearings on organized crime. There was little his high-powered friends could do—the entire proceedings were televised to the world.

In 1954, he spent another eleven months behind bars before a five-year tax evasion sentence was overturned. While in prison for a third time in 1956, another important ally, Joe Adonis, was deported to Italy. Genovese realized he had an opportunity to stage a coup and began to garner support from his young stable of street soldiers, including Vincent "Chin" Gigante.

One last major obstacle stood in the way: Mangano family boss Albert Anastasia. The former Murder, Inc. hit man was now leading one of the most powerful crime families in the country and was a staunch ally of Costello's. Unfortunately for Costello, Anastasia fell into bad terms with many top mobsters, including Meyer Lansky, when he began establishing competing gambling rackets.

With the go ahead from the top bosses, Anastasia was involuntarily retired in October 1957. Now, Genovese, after a decade of plotting patiently, was clear to make a move against Costello.

On May 2, 1957, seven months after the murder of Anastasia, Vincent Gigante followed Frank Costello into the lobby of his apartment building. As Costello approached the elevator, Gigante yelled out, "This is for you, Frank!" and fired a shot at the boss's head from just a few feet away.

The warning was a blessing for Costello, who reacted just in time, and the bullet only grazed his skull. Gigante fled the scene, convinced that he had just killed the most powerful criminal in America; however, Costello recovered. But the incident was enough to force Costello into relinquishing his position as boss. Genovese had killed and manipulated his way to the top of the family that would come to bear his name.

Frank Costello was able to keep much of his illegal interests and spent the rest of his life behind the scenes, acting as an adviser to the family until his death of a heart attack in 1972. He was eighty-two years old.

The criminal legend was buried at Saint Michael's Cemetery in Queens.

D'AQUILA, SALVATORE

91 Elizabeth Street, 1919

Alias: Toto

Born: 1878, Sicily

Died: October 10, 1928, New York City

Association: D'Aquila crime family boss

Salvatore D'Aquila was a powerful transplanted Mafioso from Palermo who ruled the American Mafia at the dawn of Prohibition.

With a record in the United States dating back to 1906, D'Aquila was a highly intelligent gangster who also seemingly happened to be in the right position at the right time. First, his outfit's biggest early century rival, the Morello gang, suffered a huge setback when its leaders were sentenced to lengthy prison terms in 1909.

Then, in 1916, Morello gang leader Nicolas Terranova was ambushed and killed by a Neapolitan gang out in Brooklyn. Not only did the Morellos

91 Elizabeth Street today. *Courtesy of Shirley Dluginski.*

Elizabeth Street, looking north from Hester Street, 1902. *Library of Congress.*

lose another strong leader, but also Pellegrino Morano, the boss of the gang that did the shooting, was arrested and eventually deported back to Naples.

With two major adversaries out of the way in one fell swoop, D'Aquila capitalized by absorbing as much Brooklyn territory as possible and expanding his operations in East Harlem and the Lower East Side—a location that would prove to be valuable in the ensuing bootlegging wars of the 1920s, giving D'Aquila a leg up on competition in this city.

D'Aquila was arguably the most powerful member of the American Mafia by the beginning of Prohibition in 1920. His influence extended to several East Coast and midwestern cities, and he had a virtual monopoly on much of the Italian underworld alcohol trade in of this city; that is, until the remaining Morellos found a formidable new leader by the name of Giuseppe Masseria.

On a crisp fall evening in 1928, the nearly three-decades-long career of Salvatore D'Aquila ended in a hail of bullets on an Avenue A street corner. Masseria replaced D'Aquila as head of the Italian underworld.

DELLACROCE, ANIELLO

232 Mulberry Street, 1914–1960s
Alias: Father O'Neil
Born: March 15, 1914, New York City
Died: December 2, 1985, New York City
Association: Gambino Crime Family Underboss

With a criminal career spanning half a century, this longtime influential mob leader was a protégé of Albert Anastasia in the 1930s and a mentor to John Gotti in the 1970s.

Born and raised in the heart of Little Italy (232 Mulberry Street was his lifelong home address), Dellacroce's first arrest was at sixteen years of age for the robbery of a local man named Antonio Derosa. Within a few years, he found himself working for Mangano family underboss and Murder, Inc. gunman Albert Anastasia. Dellacroce headquartered out of the Ravenite Social Club, where he allegedly oversaw loan-sharking, extortion and other illegal activities for three decades between the 1950s and 1980s.

232 Mulberry Street, the nearly lifelong home address of Aniello Dellacroce, today. *Courtesy of Shirley Dluginski.*

Some insiders believe Dellacroce was a triggerman in the murder of an Anastasia (Gambino) family capo referred to as Johnny Roberts, who was loyal to underboss Carlo Gambino's bid to dethrone Albert Anastasia in the 1950s. Despite his early support of Anastasia, Dellacroce somehow was able to make peace with Gambino by the time he took over the family in 1957 and was allowed to retain his position as capo. When Joseph Biondo died in June 1966, Dellacroce was elevated to underboss.

Shortly after becoming underboss, on September 22, 1966, Dellacroce and a dozen fellow Mafia leaders gathered at the La Stella Restaurant in Forest Hills, Queens (at 102–11 Queens Boulevard), in what has become known as the Little Apalachin conference.

With the party secluded in a private basement dining room and the meeting underway, police burst through the door and arrested all thirteen guests as material witnesses to several Queens County murders and organized crime rackets. It was the most successful roundup of mobsters

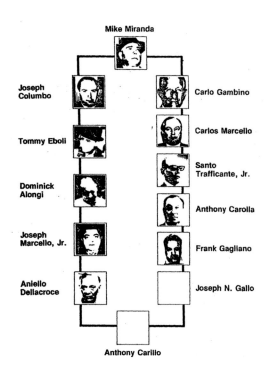

La Stella Restaurant's "Little Apalachin" seating arrangement, September 22, 1966: Carlos Marcella (New Orleans boss), Joseph Marcello (Carlos's brother), Santo Trafficante Jr. (Tampa boss), Thomas Eboli (Genovese acting boss), Aniello Dellacroce (Gambino underboss), Mike Miranda (Genovese consigliere), Joseph Colombo (Colombo boss), Joseph Nicholas Gallo Jr. (Gambino capo, future consigliere), Carlo Gambino (Gambino boss), Dominick Alongi (Genovese capo, future acting underboss), Anthony Corolla (New Orleans, future boss), Frank Gagliano (New Orleans, future underboss) and Anthony Carillo (Genovese soldier). *Federal Bureau of Investigations, NARA Record Number 124-10371-10179.*

since the 1957 Apalachin incident, in which sixty were arrested fleeing from an upstate farmhouse. Detectives said that the purpose of the raid was to "keep track of how the men relate to each other in importance within the underworld hierarchy."[21]

A hearing was held for twelve of the thirteen on December 19, 1966 (minus Gambino, who was excused due to poor health). The defense team made headlines when they accused Queens district attorney Nat N. Hentel of conducting a publicity stunt in order to further his career. One lawyer stated, "Barnum and Bailey couldn't have dreamed up a bigger three-ring circus."[22] Despite not being charged with a crime, the mobsters were held on $100,000 bail; most paid that within thirty-two hours and went free.

On November 25, 1966, local police raided the Ravenite Social Club on Mulberry Street and arrested Dellcroce, Joe N. Gallo, Paul Castellano and eight others who were out on bail. All charges were dismissed within a few hours by a night court judge because the arresting officers could not provide evidence that the group was gathered for the purpose of engaging in illegal activities.

On November 30, seven of the La Stella arrestees were called to testify before a grand jury, but they offered nothing but their names and addresses. In a show of defiance, the mobsters and their lawyers actually went to La Stella for lunch during the hearings, and the press followed. The resulting story and accompanying photos made the newspapers, and it became a public embarrassment for the prosecutors. As District Attorney Hentel became desperate for the case not to collapse, full immunity was offered to all thirteen mobsters in exchange for testimony; again, all balked at the proposition.

On May 18, 1967, Dellacroce, Miranda, Carillo and Gallo were rearrested and charged with contempt of court. All four men pleaded not guilty the next morning and were released on $5,000 bail. Eboli, Alongi and Colombo were also named in the indictment, but Eboli did not turn himself in until January 4, 1969.

Despite the media circus, the case lost steam and eventually fizzled out.

Evading serious prison time throughout his life, seventy-one-year-old Dellacroce was eventually indicted on March 28, 1985, under federal racketeering (RICO) charges, as part of an investigation that sent the top dozen New York Mafia leaders (and dozens more) to prison. However, Dellacroce would die of lung cancer eight months later, before being sentenced.

One reliable insider told me a story of how Dellacroce and Peter DeFeo were longtime rivals, and on one occasion in Las Vegas, the pair got physical and had to be separated. Stories like this are not documented and unfortunately cannot be proven.

D'ERCOLE, JOSEPH

428 East 116th Street, Apartment 18
Alias: Joe Z, Josey, Joe Morelli, Josie Romano, Joe the Book
Born: November 16, 1911, New York City
Died: May 1976
Association: Gambino crime family

According to the FBN, this portly, five-foot-seven, 210-pound mobster—whose official employment was that of a bouncer at the Delightful Luncheonette at East 116th Street and 1st Avenue—was a "controlling member" of the Mafia in Harlem by the 1950s and engaged in large-scale narcotics sales and auto theft.

Twenty-five-year-old D'Ercole was arrested in 1936, along with nine other members of the Manhattan Social Club (354 East 114th Street) in connection with the murder of gangster Dutch Schultz and his three bodyguards in Newark, New Jersey, on October 23, 1935.

Police traced a car found at the murder scene back to club member Joseph Tortotici[23] and raided the East Harlem establishment on January 7, 1936. It turns out that Tortotici had lent his car to Schultz bodyguard Bernard Rosenkrantz on the day of the hit, but since there was no direct connection with the murder, Tortotici, D'Ercole and their crew were only charged with vagrancy.[24]

In the early 1950s, a Bronx-based front for a large-scale auto-theft ring was established by D'Ercole under the name United-Drive-Yourself. Using the name Joseph Romano, D'Ercole and his associates resold over one hundred stolen cars within its first week of operation in October 1953.[25]

In 1964, D'Ercole was sentenced to twenty years in prison for heroin distribution;[26] he died sixteen years later.

DeFeo, Peter

219 Mott Street, 1910–20; 276 Mulberry Street, 1930; 130 West Twelfth Street

Alias: Phil Aquilino

Born: March 4, 1902, New York City

Died: April 6, 1993, New York City

Association: Genovese crime family capo

This "Mayor of Little Italy" was a popular longtime capo in the Genovese crime family who also operated the Ross Paper Stock Company at 150 Mercer Street and Ross Trucking Company on Mulberry Street through the 1980s.

DeFeo's parents, Giuseppe and "Mary," immigrated to New York City in 1893 at sixteen and thirteen years old, respectively. They married soon after, in 1896, and gave birth to Peter while living on Mott Street.

Young Peter DeFeo "came up" through a Vito Genovese crew based in his native neighborhood, which was led by (future consigliere) Michele "Mike" Miranda. DeFeo proved his loyalty to Genovese on September 9, 1934, when he, Miranda and three associates gunned down a man named Ferdinand "the Shadow" Boccia, a racketeer who had a fallout with Genovese over a business venture. Both Genovese and DeFeo were indicted for the murder, but Genovese fled to Italy, while DeFeo hid out at a hotel resort in Tennanah Lake, New York.[27]

The group would eventually reunite in New York City, where DeFeo continued his support of underboss Vito Genovese's quest for control of the family. By the time Genovese had dethroned Costello via a bullet to the head in 1957, DeFeo had risen to the rank of capo and would, for the next couple of decades, control his crew's operations out of Little Italy.

In October 1963, DeFeo and six other Mafioso were arrested while drinking coffee in Lombardi's Restaurant at 53 Spring Street and charged with "consorting for unlawful purposes"; however, all charges were dropped by November 3.[28]

In May 1968, Peter DeFeo, along with gangsters James "Jimmy Doyle" Plumeri and Edward "Eddie Buff" Lanzieri, was charged with conspiring to share in tens of thousands of dollars in kickbacks from union member welfare and pension plans.[29]

In August 1969, DeFeo was identified in a Unites States Justice Department press release listing the nation's top Mafia bosses.[30] Between 1969 and 1970, DeFeo's name was mentioned several times by witnesses in the public hearing of a Joint Legislative Committee on Crime investigation into the mob.

In 1979, during a two-year investigation into corruption of the local construction industry, authorities taped the president of the twenty-five-thousand-strong New York District Council of Carpenters, Theodore "Teddy" Maritas, bragging about his mob connections, including the admission of "belonging" to DeFeo, stating, "As far as Pete's concerned, you know this…the carpenters are his. Let's face it, including myself."[31]

Maritas was also co-chairman of Ed Koch's labor committee during his 1977 mayoral bid. Koch later appointed Maritas to the Public Development Corporation, a city agency that develops building projects, but in 1981, he was brought up on charges of racketeering, extortion and taking payoffs to permit nonunion members to work on construction sites. Before Maritas had a chance to stand trial, he disappeared.

Peter DeFeo retired in the late 1980s and passed away of natural causes at ninety-one.

DIOGUARDI, JOHN

169 Forsyth Street, 1920
Alias: Johnny Dio
Born: April 29, 1914, New York City (b. Dioguardi, Giovanni Ignazio)
Died: January 12, 1979, Lewisberg, Pennsylvania (federal prison)
Association: Luciano/Genovese crime family

Johnny Dio, as Dioguardi is best known, was a prominent and well-respected Mafioso who wielded great power over New York City's garment industry and was instrumental in Jimmy Hoffa's bid for presidency of the Teamsters union.

Along with his two brothers, Frankie and Thomas, Dioguardi was raised in a mob family and introduced to the Mafia as a teenager. Their father, Giovanni Dioguardi, was killed in August 1930 in what authorities called a mob-associated hit,[32] and his uncle was Giacomo "Jimmy Doyle" Plumeri, a Lucchese crime family member.

By the early 1930s, young Johnny Dio was working for a Plumeri crew as a labor-slugger in the garment industry, a job that introduced him to the politics of the labor unions he would eventually control.

In March 1937, Dioguardi was sentenced to three years in Sing Sing prison after pleading guilty to charges of extortion, conspiracy and racketeering. After his release, he spent a short time in Allentown, Pennsylvania, before returning to New York City.

James Riddle Hoffa (February 14, 1913–?) was a powerful midwestern Teamster leader who had established the Central States Pension Fund in the early 1950s, a fund that subsequently allowed the Mafia access to millions of dollars in union pensions.[33] (It is said that much of the mob's casino activity in the 1950s was funded by the illegal Teamster pension program.) In a bid for the Teamster presidency, Hoffa's greatest obstacle was the support of New York City unions, so he sought to form alliances with Anthony Corallo and John Dioguardi.

Hoffa was introduced to Dioguardi by Paul "Red" Dorfman, president of the Waste Handler's Union. Dioguardi was not a Teamster, but several influential United Auto Workers–American Federation of Labor (UAW-AFL) locals were under his control, and he'd had a working relationship with the organization since the 1930s. Corallo outright owned one Teamster local and controlled several others.[34]

Dioguardi spent sixty days in jail for tax evasion in 1954, which led to his removal from the UAW-AFL, but by December 1955, he and Corallo had chartered seven "paper" Teamster locals—phony organizations with the minimum required membership—which helped Hoffa win the presidency in 1956, a position he would hold until 1971.

That same year, Dioguardi was indicted,[35] along with five associates, for conspiring to injure a federal racketeering trial witness named Victor Riesel, who had sulfuric acid thrown in his face by Abraham "Leo" Telvi on April 5, while exiting the old Lindy's Restaurant at 1655 Broadway. Reisel was a popular labor journalist who was outspoken against the mob's racketeering operations and had finished a radio interview critical of local union leaders just hours before the attack took place.

Telvi, who was himself injured in the assault when the acid splashed on his face as well, sought to be compensated above what was agreed for the hit. The twenty-year-old hired thug apparently felt that Dioguardi, who had recruited him for the job, would be easy to shakedown since the mobster was under the scrutiny of law enforcement. Dioguardi agreed to pay; however, Telvi was gunned down outside 240 Centre Street before he had a chance to collect. All charges against Dioguardi in the Riesel attack were eventually dropped after several trial delays.

Legal troubles were just beginning for the veteran gangster, who would spend most of the rest of his life in court or behind bars. In August 1957, Dioguardi refused to answer questions from the United States Senate Select Committee on Improper Activities in Labor and Management, which was investigating his relationship with Hoffa and illegal union activity.

Over the next decade, Dioguardi faced a series of back-to-back trials— charged with everything from extortion to tax evasion—but stealthy tactics by his legal team kept the mobster from spending any lengthy time in jail until 1970. On October 2 of that year, fifty-six-year-old Dioguardi entered a Lewisburg, Pennsylvania prison to begin serving a five-year sentence for bankruptcy fraud and conspiracy. He would not see the light of day as a free man again.

While in prison, a forty-count indictment was filed on May 27, 1971, against Johnny Dio and eight associates, charged with conspiring to "violate provisions of the federal securities laws and regulations"[36] (stock fraud), as well as federal mail and wire fraud. On January 26, 1973, Dioguardi was found guilty on four of nineteen counts against him and sentenced to an extra thirty years behind bars.

Dioguardi's following convictions—April 12, 1973 (nine years), and February 5, 1974 (ten years),[37] to be served concurrently—ensured a virtual life sentence. Dioguardi spent the last few years of his life at Lewisburg Federal Prison in Pennsylvania, infamous for housing numerous high-profile inmates over the decades, such as John Gotti, Al Capone, Henry Hill, Paul Vario and Jimmy Hoffa.

DI PALERMO, CHARLES

260 Elizabeth Street, 1950s
Alias: Charlie Beck, Charlie Brody
Born: February 15, 1925, New York City
Died: [?]
Association: Bonanno crime family

Along with brothers Joseph and Peter, Charles made up one-third of the notorious Beck Brothers, suspected narcotics distributors and trusted associates of top Mafia leaders.

Charles, the youngest of the clan, possessed a criminal record dating back to 1945 with arrests for forgery, alcohol violations and burglary. His role in an international narcotics ring earned him a twelve-year prison sentence in 1959 (see Di Palermo, Joseph).

DI PALERMO, JOSEPH

246 Elizabeth Street, 1950s
Alias: Joe Beck, Joe Palmer
Born: June 8, 1907, New York City
Died: [?]
Association: Bonanno crime family

Joseph, the eldest Di Palermo sibling and reputed leader of the Beck Brothers, has a long and storied criminal record dating back to 1925 (the year his youngest brother, Charles, was born). Joseph Di Palermo is perhaps most famous for his suspected role in the 1943 murder of news publisher Carlo Tresca.

Despite the candy store front (46 Prince Street) and his slim, five-foot, six-inch, 120-pound frame, Di Palermo was at one time one of the Mafia's most feared enforcers. The FDN described him as "a most vicious criminal," with arrests for everything from liquor violations to homicide by the time his legal troubles *really* started in the 1950s.

In September 1950, Di Palermo was sentenced to seven years in prison for his role as ringleader of a million-dollar traveler's check counterfeiting operation, but he was back on the streets by 1955, allegedly spearheading an international narcotics distribution operation based out of East Fourth Street on the Lower East Side.

By the spring of 1955, Di Palermo, Ralph Polizzano, Natale Evola and several other ring members were suspected of importing large quantities of pure heroin from Europe and Cuba to the gang's plant: Ralph Polizzano's apartment at 36 East Fourth Street. At this location, Polizzano and the youngest Beck Brother, Charles Di Palermo, would allegedly dilute and repackage the drugs for street sale and then hand off suitcases to mules at Al's Luncheonette (34 East Fourth Street) or the Squeeze Inn bar (57 East Fourth Street).[38]

One witness named Nelson Silva Cantellops would later testify that between March 1955 and June 1957, he was paid up to $1,000 for each (almost weekly) trip he made to cities like Las Vegas, Miami and Chicago. According to Cantellops, the men also planned on purchasing and taking over "policy banks" in the Eldridge Street area, to use as a front for their narcotics distribution operation. He claimed that in October 1955 the gang met at Ralph Polizzano's apartment, where it was concluded that the scheme would cost between $100,000 and $150,000 and needed approval from "the right man," meaning Vito Genovese.

Some sources in the know believe Cantellops was never involved in the ring and provided misleading information to police to save himself from a minor drug possession charge. One insider described the witness as a low-level, part-time street pusher with a string of arrests for petty crimes, like passing bad checks. Following up, Cantellops was indeed pinched in 1952 for attempting to use a suspect check worth $35.42 at a deli at 104 Columbus Avenue.

Regardless, the entire case didn't ride on Cantellops's testimony: the operation was shut down when associate Salvatore Marino was arrested on a drug run in July 1957. While in police custody, Marino claims that police beat him until he was "knocked out," at which time he gave up the address of the plant under duress. Within a few hours of Marino's arrest, police raided Ralph Polizzano's apartment, uncovering heroin, cocaine and all the materials needed for large-scale packaging and distribution.

Thirty-seven defendants and fourteen co-conspirators were indicted, but only seventeen ended up standing trial, including Joseph and Charles Di Palermo, for "conspiracy to import and smuggle narcotic drugs into the United States; to receive, conceal, possess, buy and sell the drugs; to dilute, mix and adulterate the drugs prior to their distribution; and to distribute the drugs."[39] On April 17, 1959, Joseph Di Palermo was sentenced to fifteen years in prison.

Di Palermo and Genovese would be housed in the same Atlanta prison as future informer Joe Valachi. According to Valachi, while locked up in 1962, he felt that family boss Vito Genovese was out to have him killed, suspected of working with the federal authorities. On June 22 of that year, Valachi bludgeoned to death a fellow inmate he says he mistook for Genovese's go-to hit man, Joseph Di Palermo, hoping to make a preemptive strike. Faced with first-degree murder charges and the possibility of being whacked in prison, Valachi negotiated a deal with the FBI that probably saved his life, but it turned the Mafia inside out and led to revelations that continue to fascinate and terrify the public to this day.

DI PALERMO, PETER

61 Second Avenue, Apartment 3-B, 1950s
Alias: Petey Beck, Pete Palmer
Born: October 18, 1914, New York City
Died: [?]
Association: Bonanno crime family

Along with brothers Joseph and Charles, Peter made up one-third of the notorious Beck Brothers. His record dates back to 1931 with arrests for counterfeiting, alcohol manufacturing and receiving stolen goods. According to the Federal Bureau of Narcotics, Di Palermo frequented the Thompson

Social Club at 21 Prince Street and Nancey's Candy Store at 240 Elizabeth Street but had no record of owning a legitimate business.

In 1950, Di Palermo was convicted on three counts of counterfeiting and sentenced to fifteen years in prison. Di Palermo attempted to appeal by arguing that he was suffering from encephalitis (sleeping sickness) during the first trial and that he had been essentially deprived of his constitutional right to proper representation. He was unsuccessful.[40]

DI PIETRO, CARLI

21 Monroe Street, 1962; 1 Cardinal Hayes Place
Alias: Charles, Cosmo
Born: October 15, 1930, New York City
Died: 1978[41]
Association: Genovese crime family

This Genovese crime family mobster was a former professional boxer and suspected narcotics smuggler with ties to the Canadian Mafia, as well as part owner of the Vivere Lounge at 199 Second Avenue.

Di Pietro was a childhood and lifelong friend of fellow gangster Frank Mari. As teenagers on the Lower East Side, the boys invented various schemes and hustles to earn a buck, wisely seeking the blessing of the local mob first. No matter how trivial, the wise guys in training always paid tribute and showed respect. So the mob, impressed with Di Pietro and Mari, gave them permission to push small amounts of heroin around Rivington and Stanton Streets, which earned the team about $20,000 a year.[42]

Di Pietro and his old friend, Frank Mari, were inducted into the Mafia in 1957 during a ceremony presided over by Thomas Lucchese, Albert Anastasia and others. Di Pietro went to the Genovese, and Mari was recruited by the Bonannos.

Di Pietro would soon find himself involved in a major narcotics operation that allegedly brought large amounts of heroin to New York City through Canadian criminal networks. The ring, which included Frank Mari and was led by Carmine Galante, set up its plant in an apartment at 226 East Eighteenth Street. After allegedly processing and packaging the drugs at this location, large quantities would be delivered to several locations in Brooklyn and Manhattan, including the Vivere, where it was passed off to street distributors in shoe boxes and suitcases.[43]

Federal authorities caught up with the crew by the end of the 1950s. Di Pietro, Galante and several codefendants were convicted on July 10, 1962, after a colorful ten-week trial rife with several outbursts and attempts by the co-conspirators to disrupt proceedings in hopes of "provoking an irreversible error." Despite underhanded tactics and several appeals, Di Pietro and Galante were sentenced to twenty years in prison and fined $20,000 each. (Mari was the only one who avoided being sentenced; he was acquitted.)

EBOLI, THOMAS VITO MICHAEL

177 Thompson Street, 1960
Alias: Tommy Ryan
Born: June 13, 1911, Scisciano, Italy
Died: July 16, 1972, Brooklyn, New York
Association: Genovese crime family acting boss

This former professional boxing manager worked as a bootlegger in the Masseria crime family as a teenager and had become Vito Genovese's personal guard by the 1930s. Despite multiple arrests for gambling and disorderly conduct, Eboli's only recorded conviction came in the 1960s, when he spent sixty days in jail for assaulting a referee at Madison Square Garden after a fighter he managed lost a bout.

Eboli was made capo in 1957 and awarded control of the Genovese family Little Italy crew. When Genovese was sent to prison in 1969, Eboli was made acting boss, though a committee actually made decisions regarding the organization's operations.

At one point in the early 1970s, it is said that Eboli borrowed over $3 million from Carlo Gambino to set up a narcotics ring; however, the short-lived operation was thwarted by authorities, and Eboli could not pay his debt. Some theories suggest that Eboli was set up by Gambino in the first place, knowing the money could never be repaid. But $3 million is a lot of money to spend to dispose of a rival.

ng
                                    No.   8216086

Name EBOLI, thomas vito Michael

residing at 177 Thompson St., NYC
      June 13, 1911   Aug. 22, 1960
Date of birth .... Date of order of admission ....

Date certificate issued   Aug. 22, 1960 .... by the

____ U. S. District ___ Court at New York City, New York
                                  5 728 945
Petition No. 701994 .... Alien Registration No. ....

             x Thomas Vito Michael Eboli
                  (COMPLETE AND TRUE SIGNATURE OF HOLDER)

Thomas Eboli, 1960 naturalization record.

On July 16, 1972, Eboli was shot five times and killed in front of his girlfriend's Brooklyn apartment by unknown assailants driving a yellow van. This murder remains unsolved.

EMBARRATO, ALFRED JOSEPH

96 Oliver Street, 1920; 122 Madison Street, 1925;
43 Market Street, 1950s

Alias: Scalisi, Al Walker, Aldo Elvarado

Born: November 12, 1909, Adrano, Sicily[14] (b. Imbarrato, Alfio)

Died: February 21, 2001, Fairfax, Virginia

Association: Bonanno crime family capo

Embarrato was a tough enforcer for the Bonannos who, early in his career, kept a close eye on the mob's shipping industry dealings along the Lower Manhattan waterfront before getting involved in narcotics distribution and large-scale racketeering.

Sicilian-born Embarrato immigrated to New York City in 1914 at age five, arriving on the steamship *Taormina* on November 19 of that year with his young siblings, Santina and Giuseppe; a two-year-old boy named Luigi

96 Oliver, the childhood home of Alfred Embarrato, today. *Courtesy of Sachiko Akama.*

Bivona; and a thirty-three-year-old woman named Carmella Cappella. He grew up on the Lower East Side in the traditionally mob-heavy district around Knickerbocker Village.

He was neighbors with the (soon-to-be) father of Anthony Mirra, Albert, who ended up marrying Embarrato's sister, Carmella (Millie), and was listed as a witness in Embarrato's 1930 bid at becoming a United States citizen.

Little is known about Embarrato's initiation into organized crime, but his earliest recorded arrest came in 1930 and his first conviction for violation of federal narcotics laws came on September 9, 1935, with a second in 1955, where he received the minimum five-year sentence as a two-time offender.[45] In 1987, Embarrato was indicted on multiple RICO charges, along with several other family members like Joseph Bonanno, Philip Rastelli and Benjamin Ruggiero.[46]

His troubles continued in 1992, when it was uncovered that the Bonannos and top managers at the *New York Post* newspaper were working together to illegally inflate circulation numbers. Embarrato held the position of delivery foreman at the *Post* for several years (though he didn't actually punch any time cards) and was believed to be organizing the racket. A November 18, 1991 telephone conversation between Embarrato and a *Post* manager was recorded during a yearlong investigation led by legendary Manhattan

Alfred Embarrato's 1930 petition for U.S. citizenship, witnessed by Anthony Mirra's father, Albert. *U.S. petition for citizenship, Southern District of New York, no. 252179.*

district attorney Robert M. Morgenthau. The conversation implicated *Post* vice-president Richard Nasti and Controller Steven Bumbaca in the scheme, both of whom ended up pleading guilty to labor law violations.[47]

However, the relationship between the Bonannos and the *New York Post* may not have ended there. In July 2004, Embarrato's own nephew, Richard "Shellack Head" Cantarella, flipped and testified that in 2000 the Bonannos conspired with a *Post* executive to help a garbage-carting company win a contract with the newspaper. The former capo claimed that the carting company paid the Bonannos over $2,500 a month for their help.[48]

EVOLA, NATALE

12 Prince Street, 1930

Alias: Joe Diamond

Born: February 22, 1907, Sicily

Died: August 28, 1973, Brooklyn, New York

Association: Bonanno crime family boss

Evola was a veteran mobster with a lengthy record dating back to 1930, charged with everything from coercion and gun possession to narcotics

12 Prince Street today. *Courtesy of Sachiko Akama.*

trafficking. The future mob leader was allegedly present for a dinner at the Nuovo Villa Tammara restaurant in Coney Island, Brooklyn—the site of Giuseppe Masseria's murder—during a weekend-long celebration honoring new boss Salvatore Maranzano in August 1931.

Contrary to the common assertion that he was born in Brooklyn, young Evola arrived in New York City on the SS *Indiana* on June 3, 1913, with his twenty-seven-year-old mother, Francescio (maiden name Mione), and siblings Giuseppa, Giorlama and Anna and settled in Little Italy.

Evola's first arrest came while working for Salvatore Maranzano on August 31, 1930, at age twenty-three, for firearms possession. The charges were dropped a year later. His next arrest came on April 3, 1932, for coercion; again, he was acquitted. By this time, Joe Bonanno was boss of the family.

By the early 1950s, using the Belmont Garment Delivery and Amity Garment Delivery Companies (both located at 240–42 West Thirty-seventh Street) as a front, Evola became a major labor racketeer in the city's garment industry, specifically in trucking and shipping. By this time, he was working under Joe Stracci and James "Jimmy Doyle" Plumeri, before becoming a capo about 1957. Between June 1956 and March 1957, Evola had been subpoenaed to appear before several grand juries in the Southern District of New York and was one of sixty upper-echelon Mafioso who attended the Apalachin Conference in 1957.[49] (When interviewed by authorities at his West Thirty-seventh Street office, Evola said he was in Apalachin delivering a few coats for a niece who lived close by.)

In April 1959, Evola was found guilty for his alleged role in a Genovese-Gigante-Di Palermo-Polizzano narcotics ring based out of East Fourth Street, which he appealed. Drug courier turned informant Nelson Cantellops testified that he met Evola several times at various locations throughout the 1955–57 operation and claimed he was instrumental in developing a street distribution route in the Hispanic section of the East Bronx.[50]

During the appeal trial in January 1960, Evola was sentenced to five years for perjury and conspiring to obstruct justice. On April 5 of that year, his appeal was overturned, and Evola was sentenced to ten years, which he served at Leavenworth Prison in Kansas.

Back on the street by the end of the 1960s, Evola became underboss about 1968 and then, about 1970, replaced an ailing Paul Sciacca as head of the Bonanno family, a position he held until losing a battle with cancer in 1973.

FARULLA, ROSARIO ARIO

315 East Forty-eighth Street, 1942
Born: August 25, 1882, Villarosa, Sicily
Died: February 1971, Italy
Association: Lucchese crime family

Labeled a "vicious and cold-blooded killer" by the FBN, Farulla had close ties to top-level American, Italian and French criminal organizations. His criminal career began in Sicily before spending most of his life in New York City; though according to a 1968 memo, the FBI believed that he eventually became involved in a former Lucchese-run family based out of Wilkes-Barre, Pennsylvania.

By thirty years of age, Farulla had been sentenced to back-to-back prison terms in his native Sicily: four and a half years on murder and weapons charges in 1908 and two to four months in 1912 for assault and battery. Italian courts would later sentence him to life in prison for murder and theft, but he had already fled the country and settled in New York City, where his first U.S. arrest came in 1929 for bootlegging, possibly working for the Gaetano Reina gang in East Harlem.

In 1953, Farulla was convicted of conspiracy for his role in an international crime ring that allegedly smuggled large quantities of heroin into the United States from France.[51] The operation was shut down in October 1953 after being infiltrated by undercover U.S. narcotics agents. Farulla was on the run for almost a month but turned himself in on November 4, 1953, to face charges. The sting led to several arrests on both sides of the Atlantic, including that of Nicolo DiGiovanni, a Sicilian living in Marseille who was the alleged leader of the ring.[52]

According to Farulla's Social Security death index, the U.S. Consulate in Italy is listed as his last place of residence before he passed away at age eighty-two.

GALANTE, CARMINE

27 Stanton Street, 1910; 329 East 101st Street, 1930; 235 Sullivan Street; 206 Thompson Street; 134 Bleecker Street

Alias: Lilo, Charles Bruno, Joe Dello, Gagliano, Galanti, Galanto

Born: February 21, 1910, New York City (b. Gigante, Camillo)

Died: July 12, 1979, Glen Cove, New York

Association: Bonanno crime family acting boss

With a criminal record dating back to 1926, Galante earned his criminal stripes as a youth in a street gang on the Lower East Side. By the end of 1930, twenty-year-old Galante had already been arrested in connection with the murder of Brooklyn police officer Walter De Castilla and was wounded in a gun battle that also injured two young children. At the time, he was listed as working as a sorter at the Fulton Fish Market, but by February 1941, he was sponsored into the International Longshoreman's Association (ILA) union by his brother, Sam Galante, and earned a "position" at the New York and Cuba Mail Steamship Company as a stevedore. By the end of the following year, Galante had also been "employed" at the General Electric Plating Company at 176–80 Grand Street (as a handyman), the Knickerbocker Trucking Company at 520 Broadway (as a helper) and at an unnamed pastry shop at 13 Prince Street.

Carmine Galante mug shot, 1943.

By the 1940s, Galante was known to the FBI as a Mafia member and was said to have worked as a hit man for Vito Genovese. In 1942, he became the prime suspect in the assassination of news publisher Carlo Tresca, but like the many other murders Galante is alleged to have participated in, no conviction was handed down.

In 1945, Galante moved to Brooklyn with his new wife, Helen Marulli of 96 Henry Street. The marriage ceremony was held at Our Lady of Sorrows, at 213 Stanton Street. His best man was fellow mobster Angelo "Moey" Presenzano, a figure who may have played a role in Galante's assassination three decades later.

Galante was one of sixty upper-echelon mobsters to attend the Apalachin Conference on November 14, 1957, held on the upstate New York property of close associate Joseph Barbara. Over the next two decades, Galante's loyalty propelled him up the Bonanno family ladder, from consigliere to underboss to acting boss in the 1970s.

While acting boss, Galante was said to have made a lot of enemies by incorporating Sicilian Mafia members into his inner circle, leaving the other New York families out of lucrative operations. He waged a war on the Genovese and Gambino families, leading to the murders of at least eight rival family members. It is even said that he had the mausoleum of deceased rival Frank Costello blown up. By the end of the decade, the commission allegedly decided that Galante was dangerous and had to be eliminated.

At 2:45 p.m. on July 12, 1979, Carmine Galante was eating lunch at a restaurant in Brooklyn (205 Knickerbocker Avenue) when three men burst through the front door, opened fire and killed Galante and his table guests before fleeing in a blue 1974 Mercury.

Galante had undergone several psychiatric examinations over his lifetime while incarcerated, including a 1931 evaluation at Sing Sing and one in 1938 at Clinton State Prison, both of which declared him "psychopathic."

GAROFALO, FRANK

339 East Fifty-eighth Street (Midtown East, 1930s and 1940s)
Alias: Frank Carroll, Garafola, Garofola
Born: September 10, 1891, Castellammare Del Golfo, Sicily (b. Garofalo, Francesco)
Died: [?]
Association: Bonanno crime family

Described by the FBN as a "top ranking...enforcer and executioner" for the American Mafia with strong ties to Sicily, Garofalo was a highly respected and influential Mafioso, yet little has been told of his lengthy criminal career in contemporary accounts. When mentioned, he is often reduced to a footnote as a suspect in the assassination of news publisher Carlo Tresca in 1943.

Born in Trapani to Vincenzo and Caterina Garofalo, young Francesco was initiated into the Castellammare cosca as a teenager, a faction that was headed by a man named Magaddino Buccellato.

He arrived in New York City at age twenty-nine on May 26, 1921, aboard the SS *Providence*. Here, he went to work for the Castellammarese-based Nicola Schiro crime family, for whom he ran a bootlegging crew and formed lifelong friendships with the likes of young Carmine Galante and Joseph Bonanno.

After the 1943 murder of Carlo Tresca, one theory arose that suggested Garofalo arranged the assassination because Tresca personally insulted him at a social event,[53] though this is an unlikely scenario. Garofalo was never charged. At the time of the murder, Garofalo lived at and operated the Colorado Cheese Company at 176 Avenue A, as well as the High Grade Packing Company in Merced, California.

Garofalo was said to be semiretired from the mob when, in 1955, he returned to Sicily, where he attended the Grand Hotel des Palmes Summit in Palermo on October 14–17, 1957.[54] He then returned to the United States briefly to allegedly take part in the Apalachin Summit in November 1957, when it is suspected that Garofalo briefed the gathered Mafia bosses on the results of the Palermo conference. Though the outcome of both meetings is still largely a mystery, one theory suggests that at least one result was the establishment of a new heroin trade operation between the American and Sicilian Mafias.

In August 1965, seventy-four-year-old Frank Garofalo was swept up in a large-scale crackdown on Cosa Nostra operations in Sicily.[55] Shortly after dawn on August 2, Sicilian police executed seven simultaneous raids across the island, resulting in the arrests of several high-ranking Mafioso. The Palermo police, heading the operation, said they possessed evidence firmly linking the U.S. and Sicilian underworlds in a worldwide narcotics distribution ring, alleging that pure heroin was being imported from Asia, refined in Sicily and distributed throughout North America.

Besides Garofalo, seven American Mafia members were indicted, including Joe Bonanno, Carmine Galante and Santo Sorge. Sicilian Mafia boss Giuseppe Genco Russo was also charged. In all, seventeen top-level Mafia leaders were put on trial for criminal conspiracy, as well as narcotics and currency trafficking. In an unprecedented move, investigating judge Aldo Vigneri visited America in 1965 to interview several witnesses, including two FBI agents and disgraced mobster Joe Valachi, who was housed in a Washington, D.C. jail cell at the time.

Despite presenting eight years of evidence and several witnesses, prosecutors failed to prove their case, and all charges were dropped against all defendants in June 1968. Frank Garofalo disappeared from public record after that.

GENOVESE, VITO

29 Washington Square West, 1944
Born: November 27, 1897, Naples, Italy (b. Genovese, Avito)
Died: February 14, 1969, Springfield, Missouri
Association: Genovese crime family boss

Not many other Mafioso of the era quite match up to the fearsome reputation of Vito Genovese, the churlish mob leader who had no problem using violence on anyone who stood in his way. Fellow mobsters, friends and civilians were all fair game to the man who went on to lead arguably the most infamous (and powerful) Mafia organization in America.

According to Mafia insiders, Genovese entrusted very few to his inner circle and was one of the most inaccessible bosses of La Cosa Nostra. The stealthy mobster enforced an elaborate chain of command between himself and his underlings and was known to pass his own (Mafia) family members on the street without so much as a glance. Was this a crafty ploy to evade the authorities or an example of the gangster's icy personality? Those in the know think it was a little of both.

Vito Genovese mug shot.

Born to Felice and Nunziata Genovese in Rosiglino, Tufino, a province of Naples, Italy, the future mob heavyweight immigrated to New York City with his family about 1914. His first arrest came soon after—a weapons possession charge in Manhattan on January 15, 1917, that earned the twenty-year-old aspiring gangster sixty days in the workhouse, a term he served between June and July of that year.

A string of six arrests between 1918 and 1925 on charges ranging from felonious assault to homicide (twice), all ended in a discharge. Genovese would only see the inside of a jail cell once more until the 1950s—thirty days in January 1927, with which he also received a $250 fine.

By this time, the five-foot, seven-inch, 160-pound Genovese had established himself as a feared Prohibition-era strong-arm for hire and was planting the seeds of his own alcohol and gambling rackets in both New York and New Jersey with partners such as Charlie Luciano. By the end of the 1920s, Genovese had been recruited by the Giuseppe Masseria crime organization and made Luciano's underboss in the 1931 restructuring of the Mafia.

On June 20, 1930, four men were arrested in a Secret Service–led raid on an alleged Bath Beach, Brooklyn counterfeiting plant (1726 Eighty-sixth Street), where almost $1 million in suspicious currency was "ready to be placed into circulation."[56] Eight men were indicted on June 30, including suspected ring leader of the operation Vito Genovese, though he was not in police custody at the time of the indictments.

The ring was accused of manufacturing $200,000 in fake $20 notes over a three-month period between April and June 1930 and received a fair amount of press. The curious thing is that Genovese's name only appears in the first flurry of reports about the incident—but he is never mentioned again. There is no infraction listed on his police report from this time period, so it seems the gangster escaped charges.

Vito Genovese wanted for the murder of Ferdinand Boccia in 1934. *NYPD, New York City Municipal Archives.*

His first wife, whom he married in 1924, died in 1931. On March 30, 1932, Genovese married Anna Petillo, who was not exactly *available*—that is, until her husband, Gerard Vernotico, was found strangled to death on the roof of 124 Thompson Street on March 16, only two weeks before her wedding to the mobster. All gangland signs point to Genovese, though the murder remains officially unsolved.

On September 19, 1934, Mafia associate Ferdinand "the Shadow" Boccia was shot to death at the Cristofolo Café, at 533 Metropolitan Avenue in Brooklyn. While he was sitting at a table gambling, two men walked in the front door with guns drawn. Boccia's uncle, Benny, who managed the place, assumed it was a stickup and offered no resistance. When Benny told the gunmen to take whatever they wanted, one of them stated, "No holdup here gentlemen, we want this rat,"[57] and pointed the barrel of his gun at Ferdinand Boccia. It is said that the Shadow was given enough time to say a brief prayer with Rosary beads pulled from his pocket before being shot six times.

A low-level mob associate turned informant named Ernesto "the Hawk" Rupolo—who earned his nickname after being shot in the eye—eventually

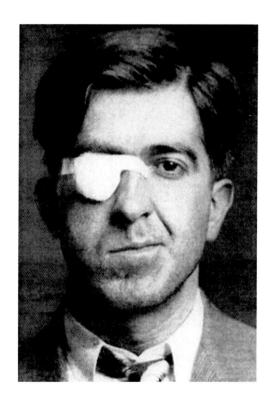

Ernesto "the Hawk" Rubulo mug shot, 1945.

Boccia was murdered while clutching Rosary beads. *NYPD, New York City Municipal Archives.*

confessed to killing Boccia. His testimony led to a murder indictment for six men,[58] including Vito Genovese, whom Rupolo claimed contracted him for the job.

Genovese, who had become acting boss of the Luciano family in 1936, when Charlie Lucky was sent to prison, fled to Italy in 1937 to escape prosecution for the murder of Boccia. In his absence, Frank Costello filled the acting boss position and would go on to rule the organization for the following two decades.

In 1946, U.S. authorities extradited Genovese back to New York City, where he stood trial for the 1934 crime. While appearing in Kings County (Brooklyn) Court on June 7, 1946, Ernest Rupolo, who served eight years for the murder, took the stand against Genovese. He testified to meeting the mob boss through future family consigliere Michele Miranda, whom Rupolo claimed had hired him for contract killings in the past. He stated that he first met Genovese at a Brooklyn restaurant, where Miranda introduced him as *don vin done*, or "the big man."

When Rupolo leaned over the witness stand, pointed at Genovese and identified him as the person who hired him to assassinate Boccia, Don Vito

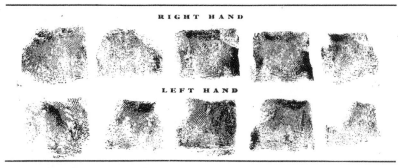

| DETECTIVE DIVISION
CIRCULAR NO. 4
SEPTEMBER 13, 1944 | POLICE DEPARTMENT
CITY OF NEW YORK | CLASSIFICATION |

WANTED FOR MURDER

RIGHT HAND

LEFT HAND

MICHAEL MIRANDI
Aliases MICHAEL MORANDI, MICHAEL MORAND and
FRANK RUSSI

DESCRIPTION—Age, 49 years; height, 5 feet, 4¾ inches; weight, 160 pounds; brown eyes; black hair. Born in Italy. Last known address 629 East Olive Street, Long Beach, L. I., N. Y. Photo Number in New York Gallery, B–129648, taken in 1919.

This Department holds an indictment warrant charging Mirandi with the shooting and killing of one Ferdinand Boccia, at No. 533 Metropolitan Avenue, Brooklyn, N. Y., on September 19, 1934.

Kindly search your Prison Records as this man may be serving a sentence for some minor offense.

If located, arrest, and hold as a fugitive from justice, and advise DETECTIVE DIVISION, by wire.

LEWIS J. VALENTINE, Police Commissioner
TELEPHONE: SPring 7-3100

Mike Miranda wanted for the murder of Ferdinand Boccia in 1934. *NYPD, New York City Municipal Archives.*

shifted in his seat and stared at the apostate killer. Rupolo was reportedly visibly shaken. He loosened his tie, unbuttoned his collar and began to sweat.[59]

A second witness named Peter LaTempa was poisoned on January 15, 1945, leaving the prosecutors' entire case riding on the testimony of an admitted killer and jailhouse rat; needless to say, charges against Genovese were dismissed. Nineteen years later, on August 24, 1964, Rupolo's body was found washed up on a Queens beach. He was shot, stabbed, bound by rope and chained to a heavy object before being dumped in the East River.

It turns out that Boccia had helped Genovese establish a numbers racket early in 1934 but felt the big man was cutting him out of a fair share of profits. The rest is gangland history.

It is said that Genovese was bitter upon returning to America and playing second fiddle in Costello's well-tuned Mafia family. For the next decade or so, he would run his Little Italy crew and breed a new generation of loyalist mobsters who helped him plot and murder his way to the top by the end of the 1950s.

It may have seemed like being family boss just wasn't in the cards for Genovese. His first opportunity in 1936–37 only lasted about a year before he was forced into exile for a decade. After finally wresting control of the organization from Frank Costello in May 1957, Genovese only spent two years on the street before he was sentenced to fifteen years in prison on April 17, 1959, for drug trafficking.

It is kind of remarkable that the family acquired so much power under the circumstances. In those two years after Costello retired, Genovese reversed much of the family's solid relationships that Costello had developed by making a lot of enemies, as well a few major blunders—like the November 14, 1957 Apalachin Conference he called in upstate New York, where police were tipped off, resulting in the arrests of sixty mobsters. To this day, many people believe that Genovese was set up on drug charges in 1959 in order to remove him from the picture altogether.

Genovese continued to rule and grow his family from behind bars through various front bosses but would succumb to a heart attack on Valentine's Day 1969. His body was shipped from a federal penitentiary medical center to a funeral home in Red Bank, New Jersey, where services were held.

Vito Genovese was buried at Saint John's Cemetery in Queens.

GERNIE, JOSEPH

336 East 120th Street, 1950s
Alias: Joseph Yanni, John Gernie
Born: August 4, 1921, New York City
Died: February 1972
Association: Genovese crime family

This Genovese soldier who provided muscle for Anthony Strollo's crew had an arrest record spanning several decades, including burglary, larceny, gambling, assault and "causing an explosion with intent to kill."

On September 18, 1957, Gernie was arrested for his part in a narcotics ring that sold heroin to undercover authorities over a three-month period. Gernie was allegedly present at several of these transactions, which were made at various West Side parking garages and cafés throughout the summer of 1956. When arrested, in Gernie's possession was a marked $100 bill used by agents to purchase heroin just weeks earlier. Gernie was sentenced to ten years in prison on February 19, 1957, and fined $5,000.[60]

GIGANTE, VINCENT

181 Thompson Street, 1928; 238 Thompson Street, 1950; 134 Bleecker Street, 1957; 225 Sullivan Street

Alias: Chin

Born: March 29, 1928, New York City (b. Gigante, Vincenzo Louis)

Died: December 19, 2005, Springfield, Illinois

Association: Genovese crime family boss

This colorful, hulking, former light-heavyweight boxer and Little Italy native earned his stripes as a Vito Genovese strong-arm before eventually taking over the family in the early 1980s. By the 1990s, Gigante was said to be a powerful leader inside the Mafia Commission, wielding influence over La Cosa Nostra organizations throughout the Northeast.

Vincent was born at 181 Thompson Street Salvatore to Esposito Vulgo and Iolanda Scotto di Vettimo, Neapolitan immigrants who were married in Italy in October 1920, shortly before arriving in New York City. Sometime after settling in America, the family adopted the name Gigante.

The alias Chin (insiders say it was just Chin, not *the* Chin) was said to have derived from a childhood nickname given to him by his mother, but it also suited him well in the boxing ring. During the 1940s, young Gigante fought in the 170-pound weight class and earned an impressive record of twenty-five wins and four losses (twenty-one wins by knockout).

Chin's lifelong loyalty to Vito Genovese was said to have originated from an incident in Vincent's childhood. Genovese allegedly assisted the Gigante family financially when he heard mother Iolanda needed an operation, and

Above: 181 Thompson Street today. *Courtesy of Shirley Dluginski.*

Left: Vincent "Chin" Gigante mug shot, 1960.

young Vincent was forever grateful. By the time Gigante fought his last professional contest in 1949, he had racked up multiple arrests and formed close relationships with several organized crime figures. His boxing manager was none other than Thomas "Tommy Ryan" Eboli, a Genovese strong-arm and future acting family boss.

In 1947, Gigante was arrested and charged with arson and grand larceny, though these charges were reduced to malicious mischief, and he was placed on four years' probation. In June 1950, while on probation, Gigante was sentenced to sixty days in the workhouse for his role in an illegal gaming scheme, which operated betting pools at several Brooklyn colleges. Twenty-one-year-old Gigante was charged with distributing betting cards at various local campuses, where students gambled on basketball games.

During the 1950s, Gigante provided muscle for Genovese's Little Italy crew and "made his bones" on May 2, 1957, by brazenly attempting to murder family boss Frank Costello in a bid by his mentor to take over the organization. Costello survived the hit, and Gigante went underground, as word that he was the triggerman had reached authorities. While detectives were staking out Chin's apartment at 134 Bleecker, they stopped two of Gigante's brothers, Mario and Ralph, who had driven by the location. Mario struck one officer who was questioning him and had to be wrestled to the ground. In the car, they found a hatchet and a baseball bat. Mario Gigante was charged with felonious assault, carrying a concealed weapon, driving without a license and vagrancy, but the brothers did not give up the location of Vincent.

Three months after Costello was shot, on August 19, 1957, Gigante walked into the West Fifty-fourth Street police station with his lawyer and turned himself in. Gigante was charged with attempted murder in the first degree and pleaded innocent. During the May 1958 trial, Costello testified that he did not see who fired the shot that should have killed him and that he had never seen Vincent Gigante before. The prosecutors' star witness, a doorman at the swanky apartment building where the shooting occurred, was painted as incredulous by the defense, and the case fell apart. (The man apparently suffered from "poor vision in one eye.") On May 29, 1958, after thanking the jury "from the bottom of [his] heart," Gigante walked away a free man. He told reporters, "I knew it had to be this way because I was innocent."[61] He then claimed to be headed back to work as a truck driver and resume a normal life; however, he returned to the courtroom less than a year later for his alleged role in an international narcotics trafficking ring.

On April 17, 1959, fifteen co-conspirators in the federal trial received a total of 162 years in prison. New family boss Vito Genovese was sentenced to fifteen years, and Natale Evola received a ten-year term, while Gigante only received seven. The judge in the trial granted Chin leniency, persuaded by a "flood of letters from reputable citizens" who testified to Gigante's "good works for juveniles in the Village."[62]

Gigante was promoted to capo of the Genovese family after his release from prison in the mid-1960s and inherited the Little Italy crew he was initiated into, which he ran out of the Triangle Social Club at 208 Sullivan Street. Here, Gigante's odd behavior began to take shape, as his power within the Genovese family grew. The former prizefighter was often seen wandering around the neighborhood mumbling, wearing nothing but pajamas and a bathrobe. His lawyers and family members declared that he was mentally incompetent; however, law enforcement officials and turncoat Mafioso claimed Chin was feigning mental illness in order to mislead authorities.

By the end of the 1960s, while continuing to base his operations out of Lower Manhattan, Gigante purchased a home in Bergen County, New Jersey. In February 1970, Old Tappan Township police chief Charles Schuh was suspended from the force for accepting money from Gigante's common-law wife, Olympia, and passing payments off to fellow officers. Gigante was accused of bribing the local police force in order to receive tips on law enforcement activities, but charges were dropped in October 1973, when the forty-two-year-old mobster was declared mentally unfit to stand trial.

Over the next couple of decades, Gigante divided his time between the crew's Sullivan Street headquarters, his New Jersey home, his mother's apartment at 225 Sullivan Street (Apartment 3D) and a town house apartment on Park Avenue and East Seventy-seventh Street. The FBI maintained almost constant surveillance on the curious mobster and, on several occasions, witnessed him enter his chauffeured town car in ratty pajamas, only to emerge at his destination suited for a night on the town. His influence extended into several profitable rackets, including shipping, construction, gambling and loan-sharking.

When elevated to boss of the Genovese crime family in the early 1980s, the elusive Gigante implemented a rule that no family member was to ever mention his name again, under any circumstance. It is alleged that, instead, mobsters would point to their chin or shape a letter "C" with their hands when referencing the boss in conversation.

Despite such tight security restrictions, authorities had built a case against the mob boss and indicted him in 1990 on several charges of racketeering, conspiracy and murder. The mental illness claim kept him out of court for several years; however, Gigante was ultimately brought to trial in 1997, largely due to the testimony of Mafia turncoats like Sammy "the Bull" Gravano.

Gigante was sentenced to twelve years in prison in July 1997 and spent the last years of his life in a federal penitentiary. A former FBI supervisor, John S. Pritchard, said of Gigante, who is said to be the inspiration behind the character Junior Soprano on the popular HBO series *The Sopranos*, "He was probably the most clever organized-crime figure I have ever seen."[63]

IANNIELLO, MATTHEW

384 Broome Street, 1930; 123 West Forty-ninth Street, 1950s
Alias: Matty the Horse, Sweet Sixteen
Born: June 18, 1920, New York City
Died: [?]
Association: Genovese crime family acting boss

This 220-pound Little Italy native was a Mafia heavyweight in every sense of the word, with controlling interest in New York's most powerful criminal organization and dozens of semi-legitimate operations by the 1970s. The Horse was a notorious kingpin of New York's infamous (pre-gentrification) seedy underworld, presiding over his empire from an apartment above the original Umberto's Clam House at 129 Mulberry Street.

Ianniello's father, Pietro di Biagio (February 8, 1893–April 15, 1976), was born in Naples, Italy, and arrived in New York in 1910 at seventeen years of age. Pietro was living at 140 Mulberry Street and had changed his last name to Ianniello by the time he married East Harlem native Michelina Zarrella (October 8, 1897–April 20, 1974) in December 1915. The couple had had their first of eight children, Oscar, in 1917. (Matthew was the third oldest.)

One theory suggests that while growing up at this Broome Street address, young Matty was christened with the nickname the Horse by neighborhood

384 Broome Street, the childhood home of Matty Ianniello, today. *Courtesy of Sachiko Akama.*

Matty "the Horse" Ianniello, Seward Park High School yearbook photo, 1939. *Courtesy of David Bellel, knickerbockervillage. blogspot.com.*

friends because of his stocky, five-foot, eleven-inch frame and impressive physical strength. Another theory claims that he earned the name after being arrested for receiving and selling twenty-two pounds of heroin in 1951, though all charges were dropped.[64]

It is unclear how exactly Ianniello was initiated into the Mafia, but records allude to the fact that he worked as a waiter for his uncle, Joseph Zarrella, in 1940, then in the shipyards of Brooklyn between 1941 and 1943, before joining the war effort. After serving a tour of duty in the South Pacific, Ianniello returned a highly decorated war hero and made his first foray into restaurant/nightlife entrepreneurship when he and Joseph Zarrella partnered to open the Towncrest Café in 1949 at Forty-ninth and Broadway. The Towncrest was a supper club where young Tony Bennett got his start, singing for "coffee and cake."[65]

By the 1970s, under Ianniello's thumb were the thriving topless bars and adult theaters of Times Square; tattoo and massage parlors; after-hours nightclubs, casinos and gay bars; restaurants and cafés; vending machine and garbage collection routes; construction and transportation unions; and even the New York public school bus industry.

With a criminal career spanning several decades, Ianniello spent remarkably little time behind bars as a youth. However, his luck ran out in December 1985, when the sixty-four-year-old veteran gangster was sentenced to six years in prison for "skimming more than $2 million from bars and restaurants" under his control.[66] The federal government took over control of Umberto's for the following seven years in an attempt to curb organized crime in the Little Italy district.

While in prison, Ianniello, along with fifteen others, was sentenced to an additional six years on several RICO counts of "labor racketeering, construction bid-rigging, extortion, gambling and murder conspiracies." [67]

Released from jail in 1995, the Horse took over as acting boss of the Genovese family by 1997, when Vincent Gigante was sentenced to twelve years in prison for racketeering and conspiracy. Freedom did not last long: Ianniello found himself behind bars again by 2005, this time for extorting a medical center. Two more consecutive convictions would keep him incarcerated until his release on April 3, 2009, at the tender age of ninety-four.

KELLY, PAUL

315 East 25th Street, 1901; 421 East 119th Street, 1908; 345 East 116th Street, 1910

Born: December 23, 1876, New York City (b. Vaccarelli, Paulo Antonio)

Died: April 1936, New York City

Association: Paul Kelly Association, Morello-Terranovas

Open up any gangster book or land on any relevant webpage, and you will almost inevitably read the story of how Paul Kelly was leader of the Five Points gang and responsible for breeding the likes of Johnny Torrio, Charlie Luciano and Al Capone.

I would like to go out on a limb here by saying that the common Five Points gang story may not be accurate. After years of painstakingly sifting through original source documents, re-creating the timeline and studying all the prominent characters involved, it is my contention that any connection between Paul Kelly and the Five Pointers has been

345–53 East 116th Street, the street where Paul Kelly lived by 1910, today. *Courtesy of Shirley Dluginski.*

misidentified or exaggerated. The person with the most enduring effect on what was called the Five Points gang was a boxing manager and saloon owner named Jack Sirocco, who somehow has been reduced to a footnote in gangster history.

I'd also like to suggest that it is unlikely that Capone, Luciano and maybe even Torrio were involved with Paul Kelly in the Five Points gang. No author to my knowledge has ever offered specifics about their relationship with the gang, nor have I seen any documentation to support the claim.

Paul Kelly, who truly was one of the most influential gangsters of the early twentieth century (but for different reasons than folklore portrays), actually organized an entirely separate band of criminals and was in fact a rival of the Five Points gang.

Even though Kelly was not, to anyone's knowledge, ever a member of La Cosa Nostra, I am including him in this book because he helped open the doors for Mafia control of New York City's formerly Irish-controlled waterfront and garment unions and worked with the mob in its formative years. In addition, most of what is written about Kelly has been misconstrued, and a large portion of his post–Five Points gang-era life (when he was most influential) is usually glanced over, if ever mentioned at all.

Paul Kelly was born Paulo Vaccarelli in New York City to immigrant parents from the southern Italian city of Potenza. He attended public schools and tried his hand at several odd jobs. By 1894, eighteen-year-old Vaccarelli was working on Pier 29 on the East River as a cargo handler.

A skilled amateur boxer as a youth, Vaccarelli began using the name Paul Kelly and entered the professional ring. On April 4, 1896, in Newark, New Jersey, in one of Kelly's earliest recorded bouts, he stopped a fellow lightweight named Gus Smith in fifteen seconds of the first round. Later that summer, on August 3, 1896, Kelly suffered a second round TKO at the hands of Tommy Dixon after being hit with a right hand that put the aspiring champ on his back. The referee, perhaps trying to give Kelly a little breather, began to count but stopped at five before dragging Kelly by the arm to his corner. Despite the help of the referee, police entered the ring and shut down the fight.

Regardless of ups and downs in his short boxing career, Kelly gained popularity as a skillful and entertaining pugilist. An October 1897 edition of the *Bridgeport Herald* praised him as one of the "fastest and cleanest little boxers in the business."[68]

Boxers were America's earliest sports heroes, and boxing was completely dominated by the Irish until Jewish and Italian pugilists began emerging from the immigrant slums at the turn of the century. These fighters were celebrated in their immigrant communities, and Kelly took the fullest advantage of his status by organizing his most loyal followers under the banner of the Paul A. Kelly Association (PKA). Like other similar organizations, the PKA, which was established by 1901, held meetings, organized dances and promoted athletic events such as boxing and wrestling. And like other similar associations, it acted as a conduit between criminals and politicians.

Kelly's boxing career wound down in 1901 as his political aspirations and opportunities grew. It is during this era that Kelly is said to have led the Five Pointers; however, again, it is my contention that this was probably not the case.

The Five Points gang was actually a separate organization made up of members of the Five Points Social Club, which made its way into the headlines by the summer of 1902. Jack Sirocco and Giovanni DeSalvio, a future politician known as "Jimmy Kelly," were early members of the Five Points gang before becoming rivals by 1905.

The Five Points Social Club was like every other semi-legitimate social or athletic club of the day—essentially a breeding ground for gangs, sort of like what AAA farm teams are for Major League Baseball. These clubs were where gang leaders and politicians alike were cultivated and trained. A 1903

The King Boxing Club in 1894. Giovanni "Jimmy Kelly" DeSalvio (bottom left) and Jack Sirocco (bottom right). Daily Independent *[Murphysboro, IL]*, *February 12, 1929.*

New Outlook magazine bluntly called the Five Points Social Club a "school for Tammany Hall."[69]

The Five Points gang recruited several street gangs to help do their bidding, including at least one that was made up of dedicated Irish, Jewish, Italian and African American *girls* as young as fifteen years old.[70]

Unlike the Paul Kelly Association, headquarters for members of the Five Pointers were actually in the old Five Points district, such as Sirocco's own saloon at 126 Park Place and "Nigger" Mike Salter's Pelham Saloon at 12 Pell Street. Their first official headquarters, as reported in 1902, was 126 White Street. Paul Kelly is not from the Five Points, has no record of a business or home in the district and is well documented to have operated out of several locations in other Lower East Side neighborhoods during that time period.

Paul Kelly's days as a Lower East Side gang leader were short-lived. The height of his reign only lasted from 1901 to 1905. For most of that time, the Paul Kelly and Five Points gangs appeared to tolerate a working relationship until a rivalry grew in 1905. Throughout this time, the police, press and public at large were well aware of all the characters and entities involved, yet original reports clearly identify the "Paul Kellys" and the "Five Pointers" as two separate organizations.

The often-repeated story of the legendary war between Monk Eastman and "Paul Kelly's Five Points gang" is actually a marriage of two separate battles. Eastman did indeed skirmish with Paul Kelly in 1904, but his war with the Five Pointers in 1902 was unrelated. Somewhere along the way, the facts have morphed. It may have just been simpler to boil down turn-of-the-century gangsterism to Kelly versus Eastman, Italians versus Jews or East Side versus West Side, as is often portrayed. (It turns out that Monk Eastman was probably not even Jewish.)

The actual story is quite complex. Except for the hard-line Italians and the Chinese, the days of ethnicity-based organized gangsterism were fading by the turn of the twentieth century. There were several multiethnic gangs that made alliances (or went to war) over localized illegal rackets. Men like Monk Eastman, Jack Sirocco, Giovanni DeSalvio, Spanish Louis, Chick Tricker and Max "Kid Twist" Zweifach were virtually equal in power at one time or another. Many gangsters switched sides and loyalties frequently. Gangsterism had become a business. And much like today's media partnerships and mergers, roles and loyalties often shifted and overlapped.

Kelly may have retrospectively earned credit for all this early century activity because, beyond Monk Eastman, he was certainly the most visible of all gang leaders. But unlike Eastman, Kelly was well spoken and a PR pro. He is often credited with becoming the first gangster "celebrity," which is not far off the mark, using this status to rapidly expand his social circle and criminal influence. Men like Sirocco and DeSalvio may have felt that Kelly was getting too big to handle and simply decided to make a preemptive move to secure their gangland future when two Five Points gang goons shot Kelly in 1905. Yes, it was the Five Points gang that muscled Paul Kelly out of his Lower East Side rackets.

It should be noted that after the shooting in 1905, it is well documented that Kelly left the petty Lower East Side gang wars behind. At that time, Charlie Luciano and Al Capone were only nine and six years old, respectively. There is little chance either of these men was influenced by Paul Kelly during this time period, unless he coached Little League on the side.

When Kelly was ousted from the neighborhood, Sirocco's Five Pointers and Giovanni DeSalvio's Jimmy Kelly gang absorbed much of his Lower East Side operations. Sirocco and the Five Points gang lasted almost another decade until about 1914. The term "Five Points gang" was then only referred to retroactively from that point on and was barely mentioned at all until 1923,

Al Capone mug shot.

when papers picked up on the story of how Johnny Torrio and other "former Five Point gang members from New York" were recruited by Chicago mob boss Jim Colosimo in the summer of 1921 to help battle rival gangsters.

None of these articles gives any specifics on Torrio's relationship with the Five Points gang, nor do later articles referring to Al Capone as a former Five Points gang member provide any details. Most original reports and contemporary biographies say Capone got his start in Brooklyn, where he was born, but glance over his supposed days with the Five Pointers in Lower Manhattan, saying that he was introduced to the gang by cousins.

Before going on to what Paul Kelly actually did accomplish in his criminal career, post–Paul Kelly Association, the following is a condensed timeline of Paul Kelly and Five Points gang activities between 1901 and 1905:

November 8, 1894: Corrupt assemblyman "Big Tim" Sullivan considers moving his association's headquarters into 126 White Street, owned by a man named John Brennan. This address (coincidentally?) will become the home of the Five Points Social Club by 1902.

July 23, 1901: In his last recorded contest, Kelly participates in an illegal prizefight in a blacksmith's garage at 207 Hester Street, facing bantamweight champion John Cucco, known as "Kid Griffo." (Cucco was later arrested for the murder of Kelly bodyguard Jack McManus in 1905 but was released.) Just minutes into the fight, police raid the venue, and a riot erupts. Paul Kelly is shot in his side and slightly wounded during the mêlée. Despite attacking police officers, Kelly is only fined five dollars for disorderly conduct.[71]

September 6, 1901: Kelly and two others rob and violently assault a man named Robert K. Bruce. Despite several witnesses, Kelly is never charged.

September 17, 1901: The Paul Kelly Association was instrumental in what is often cited as being a proverbial "changing of the guard" in New York politics. The Old World, "saloon-keeping" Irish, who had a stranglehold on politics for decades, were challenged by a new breed of European immigrants. Jewish and Italian thugs-for-hire quite literally blocked polling stations, fended off rival goons and offered up hundreds of repeat votes. As a reward, various criminal activities were sheltered, like gambling and "fifty-cent prostitution," with estimates of 750 to 1,000 young Italian women employed as sex workers in Little Italy by the end of 1901.

October 30, 1901: Four members of the Paul Kelly Association, called "One of Big Tim Sullivan's organizations" in the *World* newspaper,[72] attack Denis

McElvoy, proprietor of the Harry Howard Square Hotel on Canal and Baxter. The hotel served as headquarters of Sullivan political rival Justice Jerome.

November 2, 1901: 190 Mulberry Street is identified as the Paul Kelly Association headquarters in a *New York Times* article.[73]

November 4, 1901: Paul Kelly and associate Patrick McCabe are arrested for holding up Frederick T. Rouss of Brooklyn, attempting to steal his watch.

December 6, 1901: Kelly is sentenced to nine months in jail for assault. During the sentencing, the Mulberry Street Police Station is censured for previously shielding Kelly, whom the judge described as "one of young Tim Sullivan's friends." The sergeant of that station is accused of letting Kelly off the hook in the past and is reprimanded.

August 30, 1902: The first printed reference to the Five Points Social Club appears in an article reporting on an outing hosted by district leader Tom Foley at the former Sulzer's Park (2nd Avenue and 126th Street). About 150 members of the club attend the all-day event.

September 1902: Kelly is released from jail and focuses his attention on building up the Paul Kelly Association's membership, with its earliest headquarters at 190 Mulberry Street and branches in Harlem and Newark, New Jersey.

September 10, 1902: Nine members of the Five Points Social Club cause a small stir after losing a baseball contest at a day outing in College Point hosted by ex–police chief William Devery. The club's headquarters are identified as 126 White Street.[74]

September 29, 1902: Sixty Monk Eastman gang members raid the Five Points gang district. In the end, seventeen brawlers are arrested, and fifteen revolvers, eight knives and three blackjacks are seized.[75] Paul Kelly is never mentioned.

October 4, 1902: The Five Pointers lead a surprise raid on an Eastman hangout at 96 Suffolk Street in retaliation for the September 29 battle. Thirty-five men armed with revolvers and clubs rush up the stairs to the second-floor pool hall, where Eastman is said to be. At the end of the bloody struggle, several gangsters and police are injured, and twenty-nine gangsters are arrested.[76] Paul Kelly is never mentioned.

October 6, 1902: Alderman Tom Foley meets with the Eastmans to settle a dispute with the Five Pointers.

October 7, 1902: Foley meets with the Five Points gang to settle a dispute with the Eastmans. Paul Kelly is never mentioned.

October 11, 1902: Persuaded by Foley, delegates from the Five Pointers and the Eastmans meet at Tammany Hall headquarters and sign a peace treaty.[77] The Five Pointers then celebrate the peace treaty at their club rooms at 126 White Street. (Remember, Kelly was already operating out of 190 Mulberry Street.) The story that Foley encouraged Eastman and Kelly to face off in a boxing match to decide who would get control of the district *might* be true, though there is no documentation to verify this. In fact, despite Kelly's high profile, his name is not mentioned once in any of the original articles or reports on the gang war or the peace treaty.

February 8, 1903: Police raid the Paul Kelly Association headquarters at 190 Mulberry Street and break up an illegal prizefight between Kid Griffo and "the Creole," arresting seventeen people. The Paul Kelly Association soon moves its headquarters to 24 Stanton Street, even farther from Five Points.

March 7, 1903: The Paul Kelly Association is still engaging in legitimate sporting activities. Its wrestler, W. Gariosa, defeats W. Karl of the Pastime Athletic Club in two minutes and fifteen seconds at the New Polo Athletic Association gymnasium at 129th Street and Park Avenue.

May 14, 1903: Paul Kelly wrestles Joe "the Ghetto Champion" Bernstein in an exhibition match at Miner's Bowery Theater; after fifteen minutes, a fight breaks out between the contestants. When the dust settles, Kelly is declared the winner.

July 4, 1903: Six hundred members of "the new Five Points gang"[78] attend a day outing in New Dorp, Staten Island, with members of the Eastman gang, as part of Foley's ongoing plan to keep peace in his district. No incidents are reported while the former rivals mingle, but the Five Pointers wreak havoc as they march from the Whitehall Ferry terminal back to their headquarters. Fifteen police officers who respond to shots being fired at pedestrians are assaulted by the mob. Only two arrests are made. Paul Kelly is never mentioned.

July 8, 1903: Alleged members from an East Harlem branch of the "Paul Kelly Social Club"[79] battle police in a saloon at East 115th Street and 2nd Avenue. One officer is injured.

August 7, 1903: A Boston merchant is attacked by alleged members of the Five Points gang on the Bowery. When a police officer attempts to interfere, he is also attacked.

September 16, 1903: Paul Kelly Association gang member Michael Donovan is killed during a major gun battle on Rivington Street with the

Eastman gang. Over one hundred shots are fired between dozens of rival gangsters. This is the first time that Kelly and Eastman are recorded to be at war. No original articles mention that this was a "second war," lending more evidence to the theory that Kelly had nothing to do with Eastman's 1902 war with the Five Pointers.

September 19, 1903: Police raid and shut down the new Paul Kelly Association headquarters at 24 Stanton Street and confiscate all the organization's records. Several members are arrested on various charges, including weapons possession. Police vow to shut down the Paul Kelly Association for good. With the help of an unknown investor, Kelly eventually moves into a saloon at 57 Great Jones Street, right off the Bowery.

September 20, 1903: Michael Donovan is buried, and services are held at his home on the corner of Governeur and Cherry Streets. Several Paul Kelly Association members pay respects. On the same day, two of the association's members who were arrested during the raid on 24 Stanton Street are fined for weapons possession.

October 24, 1903: The *Evening World* reports that "assassination is a regular industry in this city,"[80] citing rates the Paul Kelly gang charged for their criminal services, allegedly told by a former member of the gang: punching, $5; punching and razor cut to face, $15; beating with brass knuckles and blackjacks, $20; sent to hospital guarantee, $50; stabbing, $5; murder, $100. The article also claimed that a pretty woman named "Shady Sadie" assisted in these endeavors by acting as a decoy.

March 14, 1904: The NYPD identifies a man named "Paddy" Brock—whom they also referred to as "Fenton"—as the leader of the Five Pointers, maintaining the position through "many successful encounters with rivals."[81] Throughout 1904, Paul Kelly is mentioned on an almost monthly basis, as is the Five Points gang, though never in the same article.

August 4, 1904: Several Kelly gang members go on a local rampage, breaking storefront windows and assaulting innocent bystanders. Over a two-hour period, thousands of dollars in damage is done, and one man, a fruit peddler named Christo Colojanes, is beaten so badly that he dies of his injuries. Police are only successful in arresting one gangster, who gives his name as William Windorf. A police officer by the name of Frye, who made the arrest, is threatened with his life and reassigned to another part of the city.

September 4, 1904: Two hundred Paul Kelly Association members gather in New Dorp, Staten Island, for an outing where a shooting occurred. One gang member is arrested; the remaining members take the Staten Island Ferry home, where a waiting squad of policemen escorts them all the way to their headquarters.

November 14, 1904: A man named John Careva is identified by the police as the "current leader" of the Five Pointers following an arrest on Mulberry Street.[82] Several reports from the era report a notorious gunman named Phil Casey as the driving force behind the Five Pointers.

March 27, 1905: A judge named Delehanty grants Vaccarelli the right to legally change his name to Kelly. Some have implied it was an attempt to woo the predominantly Irish-led unions, which Kelly had his eye on infiltrating. In the summer of 1905, Kelly is recruited to break a strike of the Cloakmaker's Union and is hired by the Musical Mutual Protective Union to assist in putting its laborers "in order." This is his first recorded foray into the labor-slugging field.

April 1, 1905: Police raid Kelly's Little Naples/New Brighton Club at 57 Great Jones, and the gang leader is arrested. He is released on April 5 to a cheering crowd of five hundred spectators, according to reports.

May 26, 1905: Kelly bodyguard Thomas "Eat 'Em Up Jack" McManus is killed in what the *New York Times* calls a "rivalry between the Kelly and the Five Points adherents."[83]

May 27, 1905: A *New York Times* article describes a feud between the "Kelley [sic] gang, who resort to the Brighton" (57 Great Jones Street), and the "Five Points gang, whose headquarters is at Salter's" (the Pelham, 12 Pell Street).

June 3, 1905: The *St. John Daily Sun* declares that the "Paul Kelly band" and "Five Points band" were "rivals for Bowery honors."[84]

August 5, 1905: The Paul Kelly gang goes on a two-hour rampage through the streets of the Lower East Side. Several bystanders are seriously injured, and thousands of dollars' worth of damage is done.

August 27, 1905: Nine Paul Kelly gang members are arrested for rioting in East Harlem.

September 2, 1905: An off-duty police officer and his associate are beaten inside Kelly's club at 57 Great Jones.

November 17, 1905: A benefit for the Paul Kelly Fife, Drum and Bugle Corps is held at Everett Hall (31–33 East Fourth Street). Outside the event, rival gangster Jack Sirocco is shot in the arm.

November 21, 1905: Members of the Liberty Association have a shootout with Paul Kelly gang members at 57 Great Jones Street. Paul Kelly is not

Paul Kelly's "Little Naples" at 57 Great Jones Street in 1905. The caption read, "Headquarters of the largest and best organized gang in New York City, the Paul Kelly's." *From* Public Opinion: A Comprehensive Summary of the Press Throughout the World on All Important Current Topics, *Volume 39.*

present, but his brother, Joseph Vaccarelli, manager of the saloon, is arrested.

November 23, 1905: Kelly survives a midnight shooting at 57 Great Jones, but bodyguard Bill Harrington is killed. The gunmen are "Razor" Reilly and Biff Ellison, identified by several news sources as members of the rival Five Points gang. Kelly leaves the scene with three gunshot wounds before police arrive and find the body of Harrington.

November 26, 1905: With Kelly on the run, a police officer exchanges gunfire with five Paul Kelly gang members attempting to rob a cigar store at 2163 Second Avenue in East Harlem. One gangster named John Gela is shot in the eye and dies soon after in Harlem Hospital.

December 1, 1905: Kelly is found hiding in his cousin's apartment at 1228 Park Avenue and is arrested in connection with the Harrington murder, though he is never convicted of a crime.

After the shooting, the headquarters at 57 Great Jones Street was ordered closed. Kelly moved to East Harlem and vowed to go straight. His Lower East Side gambling, strong-arm and prostitution rackets were divvied up among gangs led by Jack Sirocco and Chick Tricker (of the Five Points gang) and Giovanni DeSalvio (then the head of his own Jimmy Kelly gang).

Paul Kelly successfully rebranded himself as an honest businessman, and the public bought the charade. By 1906, he was registered as a junior

JOSEPH R. VACCARELLI & CO.

REAL ESTATE, INSURANCE AND MORTGAGE LOANS.
348 EAST 114th STREET.   TELEPHONE 115S HARLEM.

A SPECIALTY
of leasing and selling properties in the Italian Sections.

AN EXTRAORDINARY OFFER:

A six-story, new law apartment house on 114th Street, between First and Second Avenues, 50x87x100—23 rooms on floor: 8-4, 3-3, 1-2. All cold water improvements, subject to standing mortgages of $52,250. Rent $9,000 per annum. Asking price $82,000.

Vaccarelli Real Estate advertisement, March 25, 1906. *From the* New York Times.

associate of his brother's real estate agency, Joseph Vaccarelli & Co., at 345 East 115th Street, but behind the scenes, his influence was growing in labor unions. His ties to the American Federation of Labor are well documented, and Kelly became known as the go-to guy for union strong-arming and strikebreaking. In June 1907, the *Meriden Journal* reported that Paul Kelly hired fifty strikebreakers to clash with strikers of the White Star shipping line, causing numerous casualties.

By the time his wife, Minnie, died at their home at 421 East 119th in February 1908, Kelly had been recruited to manage the Scow-Trimmers' Union (he did not found it, as is often reported), which had about six hundred members and was headquartered at 1st Avenue and East 111th Street. Scow trimmers sorted and loaded garbage onto barges and were somewhat underrepresented until Kelly took his position and immediately initiated a strike.

On September 14, 1910, Kelly legally changed his name back to Vaccarelli. While organizing citywide strikes behind the scenes, he also engaged in several legitimate fronts, such as the Stag parking garage at 234 West Forty-first Street and a private social club called the Independent Englander Dramatic and Pleasure Club at 588 Seventh Avenue, simply referred to as "Paul Kelly's Place" or the "Club Room."

Being a former high-profile gangster, Kelly believed he was unfairly targeted by police and complained of several raids on his establishments, despite Kelly's insistence that he had gone "straight." In one case, detectives traced a car that was used in a Harlem robbery back to Kelly's garage. It was freshly painted, but of course Kelly had no idea how it got there. Then there was the occasion when police found a roulette wheel inside the club at this address. Kelly reasonably explained that he was just holding it for a friend.

By 1912, Paul Kelly may have been itching for the spotlight he had once so easily attained as leader of the most prominent gang in New York City. On one Monday night in May of that year, he essentially held a press conference denouncing his oppression at the hands of the police department. He complained to reporters that detectives were harassing his patrons and discouraging them from entering the club. As cameras flashed, Kelly claimed he wrote a letter to the mayor complaining of these abuses, stating his innocence as a reformed gangster turned legitimate businessman. However, the police department denied targeting the social club, suggesting it was a bit of theatrics on Kelly's part to muster some attention.

By 1915, under the name "F. Paul A. Vaccarelli," he was made vice-president of the powerful International Longshoreman's Association (ILA). It was here where the "former" gangster's influence was fully realized.

Vaccarelli had an immediate and enduring effect on the shipping industry in New York and had become one of the most influential labor leaders in the city. A May 17, 1916 *New York Times* headline announced, "PAUL KELLY STRIKE CAUSES EMBARGO AND TIES UP PIERS," with subtitles such as "THUGS THREATEN WORKERS" and "Employees Followed Home by Men from Longshoremen's Union—Strike Started by Force."

Over one thousand dock and ship workers failed to report to their posts at 6:00 a.m. on May 16 under the orders of Kelly. This bold move affected the delivery of thousands of tons of produce into the city from out west. According to reports, many longtime union members had no desire to strike but were threatened with violence by Kelly's strong-arm men.

Longshoremen seemingly had no reason to strike at that time. They were recently awarded a modest salary increase after threatening to strike earlier in the month: thirty-five cents an hour for a ten-hour day and fifty cents for every hour after, plus a pension after twenty-five years on the job. This was considerably more than other positions earned in any industry. Paul Kelly demanded forty cents an hour, sixty cents for overtime and eighty cents for Sunday and holiday work. When demands were not met within two weeks, Kelly forced ILA members to strike. Three hundred or so who refused orders were beaten and harassed. Subsequently, the Southern Pacific steamship line, primary transporter of dried fruits and canned goods to the East Coast, declared an embargo on all shipments from its transfer stations

Unloading banana boats in 1906. *Detroit Publishing Company (Library of Congress).*

in New Orleans, Louisiana, and Port of Galveston, Texas, which was backed up with six hundred rail cars of undelivered goods because of the strike.

Southern Pacific made no bones about Paul Kelly's ambitious shakedown. The media reported on the obvious trickledown cost that was passed on to consumers, as goods were eventually rerouted via rail. Newspapers also clearly calculated how much Kelly stood to earn from salary increases via marked-up kickbacks and "dues" from union members. Still, Kelly was somehow able to spin his image as a Robin Hood figure and retain favorable public opinion.

The strike was settled on May 21, and Kelly's demands were met. Kelly had virtually single-handedly strong-armed a major national corporation by holding an entire industry (and city) hostage. This success only raised his profile further.

Another strike in early April 1919 threatened a "Complete Paralysis of New York Harbor,"[85] according to the *Sun* newspaper; however, an internal conflict within the ILA caused Kelly to be stripped of his vice-presidency on April 19. In true Kelly fashion, within four weeks he created a new longshoremen's association called the Riverfront and Transport Workers Federation, announced on May 13, 1919, consisting of mostly Italian Americans who defected with Kelly from the ILA.

Shortly after losing his position in the ILA, Kelly founded the union trade newspaper called the *Loyal Labor Legion Review*. The first issue was largely dedicated to his removal from office, where Kelly claimed that twenty-two thousand members from twenty-two unions defected from the ILA to his new Riverfront Association. Kelly was actually brought back by Mayor John F. Hylan to help negotiate an end to the ILA strike later that year.

Labeled "Labor's Lightning Change Artist" by the *New York Times* in the 1920s, over the next several years, Kelly was hired as a consultant or "business agent" to various unions throughout the tri-state area. A newspaper reported, "MASTER OF MANY TRADES. Versatile Organizer Can Load a Ship, Mix Mortar, Carry Hod, Plaster and Lay Bricks."[86] Kelly utilized all kinds of creative methods to qualify for membership to various unions, including the time in 1923 when he learned to play the drums in order to officially join the Musical Mutual Protective Union to manage its business affairs.

In the summer of 1931, Kelly established and became president of the Loyal Labor Legion (2276 First Avenue), named after his newspaper of the same name. This "anti-union" union was considered a pioneering movement intended to "astound old line labor leaders." The legion called for "the right of men and women to work regardless of membership or non-membership in trade unions."

In September 1931, the legion sponsored the only celebration for workers when New York City canceled its Labor Day Parade due to high unemployment rates. This outing turned into a popular annual event at Duer's Park in Whitestone, Queens. Though the Loyal Labor Legion gained a lot of steam and popularity, it seems to have disappeared after Kelly's death in 1936.

According to the testimony of Joe Valachi, Kelly was doing business with the Mafia well into the 1930s, toward the very end of the gangster's colorful and influential life.

LANZA, JOSEPH

67–69 Market Street, 1920; 102 Madison Street, 1930; 300 West Twenty-third Street, Apartment 14H, 1950s

Alias: Socks, Joe Zotz

Born: August 18, 1900, New York City

Died: October 11, 1968, New York City

Association: Genovese crime family capo

Several stints in prison did nothing to curb Lanza's lengthy criminal career, which dates back to 1917 and lasts through the 1960s. This infamous boss of the Fulton Fish Market was described by the FBN as "one of the most accomplished terrorists in connection with labor racketeering" in the city.

Joseph's father, Salvatore Lanza (1865–1920s), arrived in New York City from Sicily in 1895. His mother, Carmella Lofaso (September 14, 1882–?), immigrated in 1900, and the pair settled on the Lower East Side. Joseph was born soon after Carmella's arrival; he would be the first of nine children

Joseph Lanza mug shot, circa 1940.

Fulton Fish Market, 1951. New York World-Telegram *and the* Sun *Newspaper Photograph Collection (Library of Congress). Photo by F. Palumbo.*

and take on the responsibility of head of the household when his father passed away.

In a 1920 federal census, Joseph Lanza is listed as a driver at the (Fulton) "fish market." By 1930, father Salvatore was out of the picture, and Joseph was listed as "head" of the family, living with his new wife, Rose; his mother, Carmella; and seven siblings at 102 Madison Street and working as a "delegate" for the "fish union."

In August 1924, young Joseph and a fireman named William Seavers saved two men from drowning when a group of four drunken workers fell off the pier behind the fish market. Quick-thinking Lanza swam to the floundering drunks and held two of them above water. Seavers threw Lanza a buoy and a rope and then successfully plucked the men out of the rough waters. The other two men did not survive.[87]

In 1919, nineteen-year-old Lanza got his feet wet in union racketeering at the Fulton Fish Market when he organized and became business agent of

Fulton Market, 1939. New York World-Telegram *and the* Sun *Newspaper Photograph Collection (Library of Congress). Photo by Edward Lynch.*

a United Seafood Workers local,[88] a charter of the American Federation of Labor. Shortly after, the Fulton Market Watchmen and Patrol Association was established, offering merchants "protection" from vandalism of their property or stock. Over the next decade, Lanza's influence at the market grew, and virtually every single union worker, wholesaler, retailer, transporter and commercial business associated with the fish market would be subject to a variety of extortion rackets.

For example, merchants were forced to purchase fish at marked-up prices from "approved" shipments and pay a $3-a-week tax to protect their personal autos parked on local streets from damage. Ship captains were required to pay $10 for every docking. Those who did not cooperate could not unload their boats and were refused ice to keep their inventories fresh, often forcing crews to dump thousands of pounds of spoiled fish into the ocean at the end of the day. Even local hotels and restaurants had to pay up to $1,000 a year for the "privilege" of purchasing fresh fish from the market.

Victims soon realized it was simply cheaper to pay Lanza than to go through the legal system.

The power Lanza wielded over the industry came to the public's attention during a 1931 investigation of New York district attorney Thomas C.T. Crain, who was accused of failing to prosecute the racketeers of the Fulton Fish Market, citing the fact that out of 150 cases, only 3 led to indictments.[89] At least three days of testimony centered on the United Seafood Workers, as several witnesses (as many as fifteen in one day) pointed to Lanza as the man behind the fish market extortion rackets, claiming to have paid up to $6,000 a year in "tributes" for the right to do business at the market over a ten-year period.

By the end of 1931, a network of truck drivers and fishermen from Connecticut and Rhode Island united to create the Southern New England Fisherman's Association in an effort to breach the mob's control of the Fulton Fish Market. Among several complaints was the allegation of being discriminated against for being from out of state. The association complained that out-of-town trucks could not unload without paying tribute to a New York union or hiring a union member "or else."[90] Some of the mob's retaliations were subtle on the surface but could cost out-of-state companies thousands of dollars a day. For example, despite lining up at the break of dawn, non–New York truckers had to wait and then fight for space on the loading docks toward the end of the day, when the value of their delivery was at its lowest.

Corruption charges against District Attorney Crain were eventually dismissed, but the experience seems to have motivated the nearly fallen prosecutor to take up a crusade against organized crime at the Fulton Fish Market, at least for the public's sake. In May 1933, he opened a new investigation into Lanza and his union rackets. On June 5, 1933, Lanza and fifty-three associates were indicted on various charges ranging from coercion to extortion. In October 1934, Lanza was again acquitted of all charges.

Another investigation of the market's managing practices in 1935 led to the indictments of eighty-two racketeers and a two-year prison term for Lanza. He remained on the USW payroll for a year while behind bars, until retiring from his position on December 31, 1937.

When released from a Michigan federal penitentiary, Lanza again attempted to gain control of his old union. The American Federation of Labor threatened to dissolve the USW charter if Lanza was reelected to his old position, citing a lengthy criminal record of seventeen arrests in as many years. In July 1940, Lanza was voted in regardless of the threat, and the AFL made good on its promise and dropped the USW. The troubled ex-con was forced to retire in August in order for the union to survive.

Despite the lack of an official title, Lanza remained the undisputed king of one of the largest wholesale markets in America. It is said that he worked closely with U.S. Navy intelligence during World War II, offering his intimate knowledge of waterfront activities and network of dockworkers, fisherman, boat crews and ship captains to the war effort.

By the end of the war, Lanza found himself incarcerated again on a seven- to ten-year extortion conviction. He was so powerful by then that it is said he was paid kickbacks from Fulton Fish Market activities throughout his entire prison sentence.

Lanza was arrested one more time in 1957 on parole violations for gambling and "associating with notorious criminals and known racketeers,"[91] but his nearly half century of control of the Fulton Fish Market lasted until October 11, 1968, when he passed away at sixty-four.

LISI, ANTHONY

97 Madison Street, 1927; 154 East Broadway, 1950s; 1 Essex Street, 1966

Alias: Anthony Leis

Born: July 11, 1911, Giarre, Sicily (b. Lisi, Gaetano)

Died: 1971, New York City

Association: Bonanno crime family[92]

Father Sebastian Lisi and mother Sebartiana "Neli" Grno[93] arrived in New York City from Palermo with babies Gaetano (Anthony) and Isiidora (Dorothy) on the SS *Italia* on December 30, 1912. Here, they settled at 97 Madison Street in the mob-heavy Fourth Ward district of the Lower East Side, where Sebastian went to work as a bottler at a 139 Madison Street factory.

Anthony Lisi's first arrest came in 1932, and within two decades, he had racked up multiple charges for everything from weapons possession, robbery and disorderly conduct to grand larceny, federal narcotics violations and murder. By the 1950s, he was working with the Bonannos and had close

97 Madison Street today.
Courtesy of Sachiko Akama.

ties to the Montreal Controni crime organization. He also held interest in several legitimate businesses, like the CIA and Holiday Inn bars.

In the 1960s, it is said that Lisi stayed loyal to boss Joe Bonanno during the Banana War, which divided the family for most of the decade. In July 1966, Lisi and three other Bonannos were sentenced to thirty days in jail and $250 in fines for contempt of court, a term Lisi served in October of that year. He was convicted of contempt again in 1969 for refusing to testify before a grand jury inquiry into organized crime.

In February 1971, fifty-four members of an alleged heroin ring, including sixty-year-old Lisi, were swept up by authorities during a simultaneous raid in four cities; however, Lisi was never sentenced. He passed away before the trial was complete.

LUCIANO, CHARLIE

265 East Tenth Street, 1910s–1930s; 160 Central Park South (Essex House Hotel), 1930s; 106 Central Park South (Barbizon-Plaza Hotel), 1930s; 301 Park Avenue, Thirty-ninth Floor (Waldorf Hotel), 1930s

Alias: Salvatore from Fourteenth Street, Charlie Lucky, Lucky, Charles Ross, Charles Reid, Charles Lane

Born: November 24, 1897, Lercara Friddi, Sicily (b. Lucania, Salvatore)

Died: January 26, 1962, Naples, Italy

Association: Luciano/Genovese crime family boss

"Charlie Lucky," as he liked to be called, was the legendary mobster whom many claim to be the most important in American history. That title has been challenged over time, but there is no denying the vice kingpin's legacy and influence during the Mafia's formative years.

Luciano's story has been told with varying nuances in countless books, articles and movies for over a half century; however, rarely does the author

Charlie "Lucky" Luciano mug shot, 1931.

tell you that much of what we know about this iconic mobster is essentially entirely speculative. Most of the familiar narrative was pulled together from the testimony of Mafia turncoat Joe Valachi and what was purported to be Luciano's own personal memoirs, the 1974 book *The Last Testament of Lucky Luciano* (which itself was pieced together from Valachi testimony according to the FBI, as discussed later in this chapter). Almost every word that has been written about Charlie Lucky since then has pretty much been inspired by these same sources and embellished to fit whatever narrative the storyteller is presenting.

Sicilian-born to parents Antonio and Rosalia Lucania, Luciano arrived in New York City in October 1907 at ten years old, settling with his family in the working-class district of Manhattan's Lower East Side. The future gangster icon had no Mafia ties when he arrived in this country.[94] His father was said to be a hardworking, law-abiding sulfur miner from a rural Sicilian town who tirelessly saved for years to give his family a better life in America.

As Luciano would later recall:

> *We had a calendar that come from the steamship company in Palermo, which was where you got on the boat. My old man used to get a new one every year and hang it up on the wall, and my mother used to cross herself every time she walked past it. Sometimes we even went without enough to eat, because every cent my old man could lay his hands on would go into a big bottle he kept under his bed.*[95]

In America, young Luciano attended Public School 19 (344 East Fourteenth Street, now the site of a YWCA) until about 1911, when he dropped out at age fourteen and secured employment at a local factory for a few months before deciding that holding down a legitimate job was for "crumbs."

As the story goes, Luciano's volatile relationship with his father had all but deteriorated during this time period. The future vice king had by that time already been influenced by the street and was flirting with a life of crime, spending time in juvenile detention and getting into trouble for various petty crimes like shoplifting. The tipping point was said to have come when Antonio discovered that his fourteen-year-old son was in possession of a revolver. The altercation was so intense that Luciano fled the family apartment at 265 East Tenth Street, only to stealthily return on occasion during the day for a home-cooked meal from Mom.

Spending his nights in empty apartments and pool halls, Luciano began engaging in very adult criminal activities to get by. He fell into a crowd that introduced him to the opium dens of Chinatown, getting hooked on the drug that he would allegedly exploit for immeasurable riches throughout the rest of his life. Along with other neighborhood toughs, Luciano began pickpocketing immigrants, burglarizing apartments and forming a small protection racket that terrorized local school kids. It was about this time that he began using the name Charles or Charlie—some say because people started calling him "Sally" (short for Salvatore), which sounded too feminine for the ambitious gangster.

Luciano's first adult arrest came in 1916, under the name "Charles Lucania," for the possession of a small amount of heroin that he was said to be pushing for a neighborhood dealer. He served six months of a one-year sentence behind bars, which did nothing to curb Luciano's criminal ambitions. By this time, Salvatore from Fourteenth Street was making a name for himself in the local underworld. He earned respect for not ratting out his supplier and began spending more time in the pool halls and social clubs of Little Italy. As Luciano's social circle grew, so did his opportunities, branching out from street-level heroin peddling and strong-arming to operating small gambling operations on the East Side. As mob legend has it, it was during this time that Luciano formed relationships with local racketeers like Arnold Rothstein and Johnny Torrio, who was based in Little Italy before focusing on the Brooklyn waterfront and, ultimately, traveling to Chicago to make gangster history with protégé Al Capone.

According to *The Luciano Story*, it was about 1922 when Charlie Lucky was courted by the Mafia and, more specifically, Giuseppe Masseria, who was preparing for what would become a bloody war for control of the profitable East Side alcohol trade. Luciano started out by overseeing various gaming operations and collecting kickbacks from olive oil–importing and produce enterprises, but the clever mobster rapidly gained Masseria's trust and was brought into the boss's inner circle as a trusted adviser (before reportedly having him killed in 1931).

The story of Luciano planning the assassination of dozens of old-line Mafia bosses in an underworld purge and establishing a ruling criminal commission in 1931 is not true, yet it has been packaged as fact by lazy researchers for decades. The only thing we can absolutely rely on as being accurate is Luciano's long and colorful criminal record:

June 27, 1916: narcotics violation (New York); served six months and paroled
December 15, 1921: weapons violation (Jersey City); dismissed
August 28, 1922: business code violation (New York); fined five dollars
June 1923: narcotics violation (New York); discharged
August 5, 1924: business code violation (New York); fined three dollars
December 9, 1924: business code violation (New York); fined two dollars
June 4, 1925: business code violation (New York); fined two dollars
February 7, 1926: business code violation (New York); fined two dollars
July 20, 1926: driving without a license (New York); sentence suspended;
July 27, 1926: weapons violation (New York); discharged;
October 14, 1926: business code violation (New York); fined two dollars
December 16, 1926: business code violation (New York); fined five dollars
December 28, 1926: felonious assault (New York); discharged
July 6, 1927: disorderly conduct stemming from gambling (New York);
discharged
July 28, 1927: material witness, Supreme Court (New York); discharged
August 3, 1927: Prohibition Act violation (New York); discharged
November 17, 1928: armed robbery and assault (New York); discharged
October 17, 1929: grand larceny (New York); discharged
February 28, 1930: gaming, vagrancy, weapons violations (Miami);
fined $1,000
February 8, 1931: felonious assault (New York); dismissed
July 4, 1931: apprehended for investigation (Cleveland); released
April 21, 1932: disorderly conduct, along with Meyer Lansky (Chicago);
discharged
July 11, 1932: business code violation (New York); fined five dollars
December 28, 1935: weapons violation (Miami); dropped
April 1, 1936: compulsory prostitution (Hot Springs); convicted

We do know that Charlie Lucky almost became a footnote in criminal history in October 1929 when he survived a brutal assault that left him bruised, swollen and with several stab wounds in his back. The common assertion that Luciano earned the nickname Lucky after the assault can be disproved by simply looking at original reports from the incident, which cite the fact that the police already knew of him as Lucky. The moniker was more than likely earned in childhood, as a lazy derivation of his last name.

Charlie "Lucky" Luciano arrest record, 1931.

There is no denying that by the 1930s, Luciano was one of the most influential mobsters in this city. He had formed powerful political ties that kept him out of jail and allowed his rackets to thrive. At the end of Prohibition, that meant everything from large-scale loan-sharking, narcotics and extortion rackets to gambling, nightclub and alleged prostitution operations, which ultimately landed the vice kingpin in prison and eventually deported. Historians have been polarized for decades about Luciano's actual role in the sex trade; many wholeheartedly believe it was a bum rap.

Regardless, the wheels of Luciano's downfall were set in motion early in 1935 when several extorted merchants decided to fight back against being terrorized. After hearing tale after tale of threats and violence against business owners, a New York County grand jury petitioned Governor Herbert H. Lehman to appoint a special prosecutor dedicated to investigating the city's protection rackets. Lehman approached several powerful lawyers for the position, but they all declined the offer. When thirty-three-year-old Thomas E. Dewey's name came up, the governor doubted that the young former U.S. district attorney had the gravitas or experience to handle such an operation. However, Dewey had just made a name for himself with the high-profile prosecution of gangster/bootlegger "Waxey" Gordon, and many colleagues insisted he was the right man for the job.

In July 1935, Dewey traded in his cushy $50,000-a-year private practice for a $17,000 prosecutor's salary. He had less than $300,000 at his disposal to form a team and devise a plan to take on a powerful criminal network with almost unlimited resources. Right away, he made it clear very publicly that he was not interested in low-level crooks—he was gunning for the very top bosses, which would soon lead him to Charlie Lucky.

Dewey's team of young lawyers set up headquarters in a soundproof room at the Woolworth Building (233 Broadway) and immediately made a radio appeal for people to come forward with information regarding extortion rackets. To Dewey's surprise, hundreds of tips a day came pouring in; however, most of them were bogus.

When business owners refused to talk out of fear of retaliation, he got tough, using his power of subpoena to investigate their books and force a testimonial. If business owners refused to talk, he threw them in jail. Eventually, many folded, and Dewey got the information he needed. The case blossomed into much more than he anticipated, and soon over one hundred separate rackets were being investigated, from prostitution and loan-sharking to stolen goods and extortion.

On October 24, 1935, the *New York Times* published an article naming the "Big Six," criminals whom it believed to be the top crime bosses in the country, including Jacob Shapiro, Abe "Longy" Zwillman, Meyer Lansky, Charles "Buck" Siegel (Benjamin "Bugsy" Siegel), Louis "Lefty" Buckhouse (Louis Buchalter) and, of course, Charles "Lucky" Luciano. With full support of the press, Dewey's investigation seemed to be gaining steam.

Dewey concentrated on the loan sharks first and scored a big victory on October 31, 1935, when thirty-eight shylocks were arrested and sent to prison for up to five years. Next, he turned his attention to prostitution and began large-scale raids of parlors throughout the city, arresting several high-profile madams like Cokie Flo, "Cold-Potato" Annie, Jenny "the Factory," "Hungarian" Helen and Sadie "the Chink." Dozens of drug-addicted prostitutes were rounded up and forced to go cold turkey at the newly

The Jefferson Market women's prison in 1905. Today, the building functions as a library. *Library of Congress.*

erected Women's House of Detention (now the Jefferson Street Market Library, at 425 Sixth Avenue). Many witnesses started to come forward as the investigation went on, and one name kept coming up: Charlie.

The prosecutors knew "there was only one 'Charlie'" and put a warrant out for Luciano's arrest. The gangster turned up in Hot Springs, Arkansas, where he was arrested on April 1, 1936. Luciano posted $5,000 bond, was released from county jail within a few hours and then made a crafty preemptive move to thwart extradition to New York by having his lawyers obtain a new warrant for his arrest. The strategy worked for a short time, but after several days of tense negotiations between New York and Arkansas attorneys, Luciano's lawyers failed to file the proper paperwork in time that would keep him out of Dewey's reach. Luciano was whisked from his jail cell at 12:01 a.m. on April 17 and thrown on the first train to New York, where he was met by forty-eight police officers and escorted to jail.

Taking no chances, Dewey brought Luciano to trial as quickly as possible. He was officially charged, along with twelve top-level associates, on several counts of compulsory prostitution, just hours after arriving to New York on April 18, and held on $350,000 bail. Dewey had lined up over one hundred witnesses to testify against the powerful vice lord, whose prostitution racket was suspected of grossing more than $12 million a year.

The heavily guarded jury selection process began on Monday, May 11, 1936. Before the first day of the trial ended, three codefendants pleaded guilty, leaving Luciano and nine others to face the scrutiny of a jury. Over the next four weeks, a parade of witnesses took the stand. Sex workers were offered immunity in exchange for their testimonies. Some claimed that women who worked for Luciano routinely had their tongues cut or feet burned with cigarettes if they squealed. Businessmen told tales of being forced to pay exorbitant interest rates on loans they didn't want in the first place or face certain vandalism, arson or bodily harm. Luciano remained defiant and believed he would be acquitted of all charges, despite overwhelming evidence piling up against him.

Under pressure, a fourth codefendant pleaded guilty on June 1. Luciano broke down under the pressure of Dewey's cross-examination while taking the stand on June 3. During the grueling four-hour interrogation, Luciano became so tripped up by the prosecutor's barrage of questions that he admitted to just about everything *but* running the prostitution ring. The flustered gangster was forced to admit that he had lied under oath, sold narcotics, was a former bootlegger, organized gambling operations, failed to pay taxes (ever) and much more, but he would not bend on the prostitution charges. Luciano also admitted to knowing Giuseppe Masseria, Louis Buchalter, Jacob Shapiro, Benjamin Siegel and others but denied any association with veteran criminal Ciro Terranova, even when faced with the record of several phone calls placed from Luciano's hotel room to the "Artichoke King's" private phone number.

The case came to an end after four weeks, on June 6, 1936, and it took the jury only six hours to deliberate Luciano's fate. He was found guilty on sixty-two out of ninety counts against him and sentenced to thirty to fifty years in prison on June 18.

A scathing probation report accompanied the conviction, citing Luciano as "a shallow and parasitic individual" with "average intelligence," whose "social outlook is essentially childish." It went on to explain that his only real leadership quality was essentially bravado and that he "manifests a peasant-like faith in chance and has developed an attitude of nonchalance. His behavior patterns are essentially instinctive and primitive, his manner easy, copious and ingratiating."[96]

Luciano's fabled influence from behind bars during World War II has been debated over the years. The mob's relationship with naval intelligence is well documented but to what extent is left to speculation. As gangland legend maintains, the U.S. government recruited the incarcerated gangster for his support in the war effort; and in exchange for special treatment, Luciano and the mob helped secure the waterfront and used their connections in Sicily to ensure a smooth Allied invasion. However, Luciano would later play down his role as minimal and a "sham."

Another theory purports that the underworld actually manufactured a homeland security threat by setting ablaze the captured SS *Normandie* docked in New York Harbor on February 9, 1942, and then bamboozled the government into recruiting its services.

Regardless of circumstances, after almost a decade behind bars, Luciano's sentence was commuted on January 3, 1946—because of his assistance during the war campaign—with the stipulation that he be deported to Italy and never return to America. On February 2, 1946, the exiled mobster was transferred to Ellis Island, where he waited five weeks while deportation arrangements were made. During that time, Luciano was visited by Albert Anastaia, Meyer Lansky and Frank Costello, who passed Luciano $2,500 in traveler's checks and a suitcase full of clothing and gifts.

Luciano was moved to Pier 7 in Brooklyn on February 8 and placed in a five- by eight-foot cabin aboard the SS *Laura Keene*, the seven-thousand-ton cargo freighter that would return him to his homeland. Despite being under twenty-four-hour guard by six Immigration and Naturalization Service (INS) agents, the FBI believed that an unauthorized going-away party was held for Luciano on the ship in the hours before his departure on February 10. On February 28, 1946, after a seventeen-day voyage, Charlie Lucky stepped foot on Italian soil in Naples, where he was briefly interrogated by local carabinieri and sent straight to Palermo.

According to biographers, Luciano was not content in Sicily and returned to the Italian mainland soon after arriving, spending time in luxurious hotels throughout Naples and Rome before making trips out of the country to Mexico and the Caribbean.

Charlie Lucky and childhood friend Meyer Lansky were said to have called a historic underworld meeting in Havana, Cuba, in December 1946. Luciano secured his visa through a corrupt Cuban official who held interest in a mob-funded racetrack and casino on the island. In attendance at what would become known as the Havana Conference were dozens of upper-echelon mobsters from several North American cities. Rumored to have been discussed during the weeklong convention was, among other things, the establishment of a large-scale narcotics trade between the North American Mafia and Italian Cosa Nostra organizations.

When United States officials became aware of Luciano's presence in the Caribbean, they put the squeeze on Cuba to deport him, eventually recruiting the help of President Truman, who threatened to halt all medical aid to the tiny island unless it complied. On February 22, 1947, Luciano was arrested and held until he was deported back to Italy on March 20, 1947.

The exiled vice king lived his final years in the lap of luxury—vacationing in the poshest resorts and giving interviews, signing autographs and working on a biopic of his life with Hollywood producer Martin Gosch. Luciano began making some startling confessions, like the allegation that his release from U.S. prison in 1946 had nothing to do with him assisting the government, claiming instead that he had sensitive information about a prominent official and threatened to go public with it if not released.

While meeting Gosch at Naples International Airport on January 26, 1962, Luciano collapsed and died of a heart attack at the age of sixty-four. The underworld did not seem too pleased that plans for the Luciano movie were moving forward, as several people associated with the project received death threats, including Cameron Mitchell, who was set to portray Lucky in the leading role. In February 1962, the actor claimed that he had received three threatening letters written in "very bad English."[97] The movie was never made; however, Gosch told Charlie Lucky's story in the 1974 book *The Last Testament of Lucky Luciano*.

In a surprising twist, on February 5, 1962, the Roman newspaper *Telesera* ran an article entitled, "Lucky Luciano lavorava per l'FBI." ("Lucky Luciano Was Working for the FBI"). This startling claim was made by former Luciano bodyguard Bill Mancuso, who also alleged that Martin Gosch was a federal agent taking on the guise of a movie producer. To throw another wrench into the story, Gosch was quoted in a February 23, 1962 Madrid daily, *ABC*, as believing that Luciano had been poisoned. He stated, "He appeared as though he were drugged."

Oddly, the first two pages of a February 1962 FBI internal report on the relationship between Luciano and Gosch, made available to the public through the Freedom of Information Act, are almost completely redacted.

On the third page, the feds offer their version of Luciano's death, disputing the growing speculation that he was assassinated. According to the memo, Luciano collapsed just minutes after meeting Gosch at the Naples airport. Gosch happened to know that the gangster carried medication for a heart condition and "frantically searched" Luciano's pockets, where he found a pillbox, and then "removed one of the pills and placed it in Luciano's mouth." They purported that those who witnessed the incident sparked the poisoning conspiracy.

An October 2, 1974 FBI memo trashed *The Last Testament of Lucky Luciano*, citing several historical inaccuracies and raising doubts about the author's integrity. The chief of the U.S. Narcotics Bureau in Rome called Gosch "a liar," "untrustworthy" and "an opportunist." Beyond the alleged discrepancies, authorities bluntly argued the fact that if Gosch really did have in his possession the "secret memoirs" of Lucky Luciano, "it is inconceivable" that he "would still be alive today."

To sum up what the federal authorities believe about the book that has influenced thousands of authors, journalists and movie and television producers over the last four decades: "It is not believed that this book has any value to the FBI, or to anyone for that matter."

Salvatore Lucania's body was entombed at St. John's Cemetery in Queens, New York.

MARI, FRANK

373 Broome Street, 1942; 124 Forsyth Street, 1957; 20 Monroe Street, 1962; 68 Forsyth Street

Alias: Frankie T, T, Frank Russo

Born: July 27, 1926, Reggio di Calabria, Italy[98] (b. Mari, Francesco)

Died: April 1981, Brooklyn, New York

Association: Bonanno crime family underboss

Very little has been written about Mari, a very influential yet notoriously reclusive Mafioso who stayed out of the spotlight for most of his criminal career. Despite being a suspect in two murders, a federal narcotics indictment that sent thirteen of his associates up the river and several arrests dating back

373 Broome Street today. *Courtesy of Sachiko Akama.*

to 1945, Mari only spent three months of his life behind bars—on a gun charge in 1968.

He was said to be a quiet, reserved and utterly unassuming mobster who preferred quiet evenings at home collecting coins or spending time with his family and dog to partying with the boys at noisy nightclubs and unfamiliar restaurants. According to Nicolas Pileggi's excellent *New York Times* magazine article entitled "The Story of T" (March 29, 1970), Mari was the kind of guy who did not flex his Mafia muscle in his private life; he stood in line at the movies and took verbal abuse from retail clerks like everyone else. Only on occasion did Mari take advantage of his position at home, like the time he had a non-mob drug pusher "mercilessly" beaten at the request of a friend for selling drugs too close to a neighborhood school.

Eight-year-old Franceso Mari arrived in New York City from Naples with his older sisters, Domenica (twenty-five years old), Antonia (sixteen) and Adelina (fifteen), aboard the SS *Conte Di Savoia* on January 17, 1935. Father Matteo and mother Concetta De Franco had been in New York City for several years before their children joined them, making at least three trips back to Italy during the interim.

Mari grew up on Broome Street in the heart of Little Italy, where his father is recorded as working at Macy's department store on Thirty-fourth Street. After only two years of high school, Mari, now living in Knickerbocker Village, teamed up with neighborhood pal Carli Di Pietro to organize a variety of neighborhood hustles, eventually basing operations out of a sandwich shop on Rutgers and Cherry Streets.

Mari understood the code of the streets at a young age. Even as a teenager, he knew he would get nowhere without the backing of the local mob, so he was sure to get its blessing before any endeavor and always kicked back a tribute. This show of respect impressed local Mafioso like Carmine Galante, who virtually took Mari under his wing and bred him for a life in the Mafia.

At twenty-one, Mari married Di Pietro's sister, Mildred. By that time, with the help of Galante and others, Mari allegedly branched out into loan-sharking, narcotics sales, gambling and murder-for-hire. Since he was from a "civilian" family—that is, he had no previous Mafia connections—Mari felt he had to work harder to gain a position in a mob family. It is said that he never turned down a job and showed a great deal of respect to his handlers, showing up at every funeral or ceremony and keeping out of petty disputes. Before long, Mari was overseeing a number of diverse operations, contracting out assignments to crews of hit men, jewelry thieves, racketeers and burglars. He also expanded his horizons and acquired interest in several legitimate businesses, including a handful of discount appliance stores.

Frank Mari and Carli Di Pietro were made in 1956 at a ceremony presided over by Thomas Lucchese and Albert Anastasia, held in a basement of an Elizabeth, New Jersey home. It is said that the Luccheses also wanted to recruit Mari, but his sponsor, Carmine Galante, had the right to first pick. (His partner and childhood friend, Carli Di Pietro, was initiated into the Genovese family.)

In August 1957, Mari was arrested with three others for the petty crime of robbing $300 worth of costume jewelry from an automobile, though they were never sentenced. In June 1962, Mari was the only mobster out of fourteen to be acquitted in a federal narcotics violation trial that sent Galante and Di Pietro to prison for several years.

Mari turned out to be one of the best earners the mob had, with an ever-expanding influence in a wide variety of operations: construction sites, beauty parlors, barber supply manufacturers, bowling alleys, pizza stands, craps games—you name it. By the 1960s, Mari was one of the Bonannos' most trusted and respected members. His even temper and fair judgment made him a trusted adviser to many, and he was called in several times to settle conflicts. It is said that he was ultimately made responsible for overseeing certain important family operations, like police payoffs and bail arraignments.

With all his success, Mari moved his family to a quiet suburb in Nassau County, Long Island, and attempted to live a normal middle-class life, even putting his son through medical school. At the height of his criminal career, Mari must have thought his life was set. However, his world came crashing down in 1964 after a conversation with Joe Bonanno. The boss asked Mari to support him in his war against the Mafia Commission—a frightening proposition for even the most steely killer—and Mari was backed into a corner. He knew too much about Bonanno and rightly suspected that he would become a primary target no matter which path he chose.

Mari chose to side with the commission. The Bonannos split into a camp that supported Bonanno and a camp that supported the newly commission-appointed boss, Gaspar Di Gregorio, who directed Mari to make a preemptive strike on the Bonanno loyalist movement.

In the spring of 1964, Mari allegedly organized a failed hit on Bonanno's son, Salvatore "Bill." In retaliation, Mari was shot and wounded in a Brooklyn ambush in July of that year. In November 1967, three of Mari's men were gunned down by machine gun in a Queens restaurant. In the spring of 1968, Bonanno associate Sam Perrone was killed by two men police believed to be Mari and his bodyguard, James Episcopia. Charges in the murder were never filed, but Mari was caught with a gun a few days later and sent to prison for three months. (Authorities believed Mari was staking out another target when they picked him up.)

Not long after serving his sentence, Mari and two of his closest associates simply, and suspiciously, disappeared. No bodies were ever found, missing persons' reports were not immediately filed and no funeral was ever arranged, leading many to believe the men went into hiding. Another theory is that Mari flipped and went into witness protection to ensure his safety, though those who knew him would probably find that hard to believe.

Masseria, Giuseppe

80 Second Avenue, 1920s
Alias: the Boss
Born: 1887, Trapani, Sicily
Died: April 15, 1931, New York City
Association: Morello, Masseria crime families

This address was the home of one of the Prohibition era's most pivotal crime figures, Giuseppe Masseria, whose ambition to dominate the Italian underworld earned him the ultimate pink slip in 1931.

With Giuseppe Morello sentenced to prison in 1909 and his replacement, Nicolas Terranova, gunned down in 1916, the fate of the deteriorating and splintered Morello gang eventually fell into the hands of the rotund, abrasive, thirty-something-year-old veteran criminal who went on to assemble an impressive stable of up-and-coming gangsters and reclaim much of the gang's clout. It was Masseria who introduced Charlie Luciano to the Mafia

80 and 82 Second Avenue today. *Courtesy of Shirley Dluginski.*

Giuseppe Morello mug shot.

in the early 1920s, and it was Masseria's war with Salvatore Maranzano that inadvertently led to the restructuring of the Mafia in 1931.

Charlie Luciano took over the organization in 1931, with Vito Genovese as his underboss and Frank Costello as consigliere. The Masseria/Luciano outfit would forever become known as the Genovese family after the testimony of Joe Valachi in the early 1960s.

MATRANGA, PASQUALE

125 East Fourth Street, 1940s
Alias: Patsy, Matranca
Born: November 1, 1887, Monreale, Sicily
Died: [?]
Association: [?]

This influential yet low-profile mobster left little trace of his activities and is somewhat of a mystery. Though no criminal record exists in the United States or Italy, the FBN alleged Matranga was a major narcotics smuggler with Mexican and European criminal ties, and historians suggest he was one of Charlie Luciano's closest associates.

There is an SS *Laconia* passenger list record dated May 18, 1914 with a Pasquale Matranga that fits the gangster's description, but it is difficult to confirm that this is him. The FBN claims he was naturalized in the Bronx on March 23, 1928. We do know Mantranga was a partner in something called the Garden State Lathe Company in Palisades, New Jersey, and also operated a small olive oil and cheese store in Brooklyn at 8733 Twenty-third Avenue. Beyond that, most of what can be found about this enigmatic figure comes from an incident where Matranga personally delivered an American automobile to an exiled Charlie Luciano in 1948.

On June 26, 1951, Matranga testified before a Senate committee investigating the underworld narcotics trade. Translated through daughter Maria de Auria, the mobster was questioned about the 1948 white Oldsmobile sedan in question (with New Jersey license plates RUX-37), explaining that he was planning a visit back to his homeland to see family when a mutual friend named Tony Sabio asked him to transport the car as a favor. According to Matranga, Sabio had given him enough money for the car (which cost $2,783) and expenses to ship it to Italy. Once overseas, Luciano drove it from the port and registered it in his name the same day. Both Luciano and Matranga were indicted for importing a car without a license.

MAURO, VINCENT

22 King Street; 155 East Fifty-seventh Street, 1962
Alias: Vinny Bruno, Morrow Morrio, Murio, Maurio
Born: February 26, 1916, New York City (b. Mauro, Vincenzo Francesco Angelo)
Died: [?]
Association: Genovese crime family

Described as a "high-ranking" member of a Genovese crew led by Anthony Strollo, the authorities believed Mauro to be a "merciless and vicious killer" with interests in various rackets like nightclubs, loan-sharking, labor racketeering and drug trafficking.

Mauro grew up at 691 East 230th Street in the Bronx, where his first arrest came in 1933 at the tender age of seventeen. Next came a string of arrests for robbery, burglary, tax evasion, narcotics violations, homicide and a few stints behind bars.

While living at 3824 Bronx Boulevard in 1934, Mauro was arrested for the killing of a twenty-eight-year-old petty gambler and "known hoodlum" named Rocco Loscalzo of 312 West Twentieth Street. Loscalzo, who was out on bail for stealing a truck filled with $20,000 worth of merchandise from a Brooklyn warehouse, was shot five times in the head and five times in the back on October 24 after leaving a place called DeMartino's Bar at 171 Bleecker Street. Mauro was picked up soon after the shooting by two detectives while sitting in his car on West Sixty-fifth Street between Central Park West and Broadway. He denied involvement, despite the fact that his clothing was stained with blood.

In May 1957, Mauro and three associates pleaded guilty to "possessing liquor with intent to sell without a license" from their "high-class speakeasy," the Gold Key Club at 26 West Fifty-sixth Street.[99]

In May 1961, Mauro and sixteen others were rounded up and arrested, accused of running a multimillion-dollar narcotics ring responsible for smuggling over two hundred pounds of heroin into North America from Italy by allegedly using unsuspecting immigrants as mules.

The ring, headed by Mauro, was said to have moved over $50 million in heroin in just a one-year period. Rather than face trial, Mauro and partners Frank Caruso and Salvatore Maneri fled to Europe, where U.S. narcotics agents tracked them to Barcelona, Spain, and arrested the trio in January 1962.

Soon after the arrest, it came to light that authorities had been building a case against Charlie Luciano for his alleged role in the international narcotics ring. American agents tied Luciano to Mauro, Caruso and Maneri through a man named Henry Rubino, Mauro's partner in New York and Miami nightclubs. Rubino was observed making several trips between Luciano's home in Naples, Italy, and Mauro's Barcelona hideout.

The entire case was triggered by the October 1960 arrest of four men in Westchester County, New York, who were in possession of twenty-three and a half pounds of heroin, with a street value of $3 million.

MIRRA, ANTHONY

106 Madison Street, 1930; 115 Madison Street, 1957
Alias: Mirro
Born: July 18, 1927, New York City
Died: February 18, 1982, New York City
Association: Bonanno crime family

Anthony Mirra was a notoriously hot-tempered hit man for the mob with a record dating back to 1948 for a variety of charges, including assault, weapons and narcotics violations and contempt of court for throwing a wooden chair at a prosecutor during a federal trial in 1962.

In a great example of how Mafia legends snowball, several contemporary sources such as Wikipedia (as of this writing) cite Mirra as "6'3" and 230 pounds" with "sixty murders" under his belt. The FBN lists him at "6'0" and 210 pounds," while articles in the 1960s describe him as having a "stocky, 5'10" frame." The truth about his stature is probably somewhere in the middle; however, "sixty murders" is quite farfetched and highly unlikely.

Mirra's father, Albert, emigrated from Benevento, Italy, to New York City in 1912 at about fifteen years old. Here, he became friendly with the family of neighbor and future mobster Alfred Embarrato and ended up marrying Embarrato's sister, Carmella (known as "Millie"). Anthony was born in 1927 and raised at 106 Madison Street in the heart of the Fourth Ward on the Lower East Side.

It is said that Mirra was distant and reclusive as a child and had very few close, personal friends. Random mood swings, unprovoked outbursts and unpredictable violence kept family and fellow mobsters at arm's length throughout Mirra's life and earned him many enemies.

One thing that kept Mirra in good light with the Mafia was the fact that he was a dedicated and interminable earner. His icy personality, said to be void of any resemblance of empathy or compassion, helped Mirra become one of the most feared and successful extortionists and racketeers of the 1970s, though he hit a few major speed bumps along the way.

In September 1957, Mirra was one of forty-six defendants and sixteen co-conspirators indicted for allegedly operating a massive $20 million-a-year heroin and cocaine syndicate that smuggled up to fifty pounds of narcotics

Knickerbocker Village, the corner of Madison and Market Streets today. *Courtesy of Sachiko Akama.*

into the United States from France at a time. The multiethnic ring established several distribution points across North America, including Massachusetts; Washington, D.C.; Maryland; Pennsylvania; Louisiana; Texas; California; Florida; and Montreal. It was funded by gambler and racketeer Harry "Nig Rosen" Stromberg, a close associate of Frank Costello and Meyer Lansky and a veteran labor slugger who earned his criminal stripes as a hired gun for the notorious Lepke-Gurrah outfit of the 1920s and '30s.

Stromberg was sentenced to five years in April 1958. Mirra, while free on bail awaiting an appeal, was spotted having dinner at Marino's Restaurant (716 Lexington Avenue) with Anthony Strollo, Vincent Mauro and Luciano gunman Anthony "Little Augie Pisano" Carfano just forty-five minutes before Carfano was gunned down on a Forest Hills, Queens street. Mirra was questioned, but no charges were filed.

Mirra was eventually convicted for his part in the Stromberg narcotics ring and began serving a three-and-a-half-year sentence at the end of 1958.

While incarcerated on those charges, Mirra was named in another narcotics violations indictment, along with Carmine Galante, Carli Di Pietro and several others. The ring was allegedly led by Giovanni "Big John" Ormento, a powerful Lucchese capo and brother-in-law of John Dioguardi.

This trial began on November 21, 1960, and lasted six months, ending in a mistrial after the jury foreman "broke his back in an unexplained fall down a flight of stairs in an abandoned building in the middle of the night."[100] At least one government witness claimed to receive death threats during the trial, and several jury members were dismissed for various unverifiable reasons, like illness or prejudice. The judge refused to set bail while prosecutors prepared an appeal, announcing that the defendants "would be a danger to the public, to the witnesses, to the jurors and to court personnel."[101]

Mirra and his thirteen codefendants remained behind bars until the retrial in April 1962. This trial turned out to be more colorful than the first and was beset by several sensational outbursts and interruptions. In May 1962, two codefendants, Carmine and Salvatore Panico, attempted to intimidate the jury by standing up from their chairs and shouting at them; Salvatore climbed into the jury box and began pushing around a jurist. The Panico brothers were gagged and chained to their chairs for over a week after the incident.

One week later, on June 4, Mirra stood up from the witness stand while being cross-examined and, without a word, picked up the fifteen-pound wooden chair he was sitting on and hurled it at assistant U.S. attorney John Rosner. Mirra was tackled by four officers and bound by shackles. On June 8, the trial was temporarily adjourned when Salvatore Panico slit his wrists in a Federal House of Detention cell (427 West Street).

Mirra, Galante, Di Pietro, Ormento and nine others were sentenced on July 10, 1962, to a total of 276 years in prison. Mirra, Galante and Di Pietro received 20-year sentences, while ringleader Ormento was hit the hardest, with a hefty 40-year sentence. Mirra, Galante and six others were awarded additional sentences of up to eighteen months for contempt of court. Appeals by Mirra in 1963 and 1967 were unsuccessful.

Anthony Mirra was back on the street by the early '70s. Spending over a decade behind bars did little to dissuade the ex-con from engaging in organized crime, and he began a large-scale shakedown racket of Manhattan nightclubs, bars and restaurants. Working under Bonanno capo Michael Zaffarano, Mirra became involved in the adult film industry (behind the scenes) and provided muscle in the Bonanno-controlled porn theaters of Times Square.

In October 1974, a Bangladeshi immigrant and restaurateur named Shamsher Wadud provided the public a firsthand account of how a Mafia shakedown is carried out, via an article in the *New York Times*.[102] Wadud opened a discotheque called Nirvana Culture at 151 East Fiftieth Street and claimed that within two weeks three men walked in and offered to help increase business. A man introduced as Anthony Graziano (a Lucchese family member) told Wadud, "You've got a terrific place here...But you should be doing a lot more business than this. Give us a call. We can do a lot to help you."

Wadud did not call, and two days later over a dozen men entered the club and began to harass the patrons. An associate of Graziano told Wadud, "This kind of problem can happen all the time. When you wind up in the hospital, you'll wish you had called us."

The very next day, Wadud met with Graziano and company, who offered to increase his business from $7,000 to $25,000 a week for 10 percent of the profits. He explained to the naïve club owner, "This is not a shakedown, just give us a chance." Wadud agreed, and sure enough patronage increased almost immediately. Only there was a problem: the crowd was composed of mob associates who ran up large tabs, refused to pay their bills, got into fights and drove away regular customers.

As (bad) luck would have it, Wadud was soon approached by Anthony Mirra, who demanded a whopping 50 percent of profits from the discotheque. Wadud went to his new partner, Anthony Graziano, who essentially offered to keep Mirra off his back for 25 percent of the club's profits. Instead of dealing with the headache, Wadud closed Nirvana within a few days and went into hiding. Such was the cost of doing business in 1970s New York City.

In March 1977, Anthony Mirra met a man who introduced himself as a jewel thief named Donnie Brasco, unknowingly setting in motion the near collapse of the Bonanno crime family. Thanks to Hollywood, the story of undercover FBI special agent Joseph Pistone, aka Donnie Brasco, has been well told. But unfortunately for Mirra, he would not live to see the movie.

On February 18, 1982, a woman complained to police that a gray Volvo was blocking the garage entrance to Independence Plaza, a residential apartment building at 80 North Moore Street. Upon investigation, the engine was still running, and Mirra's body was found slumped over with four bullet wounds to the back of his head and $10,000 in his pocket.

Mirra's murder is said to have been orchestrated by his own uncle, Alfred Embarrato, and carried out by cousins Joey D'Amico and Richie Cantarella on the orders of Bonanno boss Joe Massino. It was retaliation for Mirra allowing the FBI infiltration.

Morello, Giuseppe

178 Christie Street, 1903; 630 East 138th Street, 1909; 207 East 107th Street, 1910

Alias: Piddu, Peter Morello, Clutch Hand

Born: May 2, 1867, Corleone, Sicily

Died: August 15, 1930, New York City

Association: Founder of the Morello gang

At the turn of the century, Morello organized a band of Sicilian extortionists and counterfeiters in New York City, unknowingly planting the seeds of

Giuseppe Morello sketch. *"My Ten Biggest Man Hunts" article by William J. Flynn, former chief of the United States Secret Service. Published in the New York Herald, January 29, 1922.*

what would become known as the "First Family of the American Mafia," an organization the FBI would christen the "Genovese crime family" in the 1960s.

In 1872, when Morello was a child back in Sicily, his father, Cologero Morello, died, leaving his son in the care of young mother Angela Piazza Morello. In 1876, Angela remarried, to a man named Bernardo "Beney" Terranova (July 6, 1847–May 28, 1913), who had three sons of his own: Ciro, Vincenzo and Nicolas.

When the Morello-Terranova stepbrothers became teenagers, Bernardo, a member of the Sicilian Fratelanza himself, encouraged them to join the local Cosca before moving the family to the United States in 1893.

The Terranovas initially settled on the Lower East Side,[103] before family members branched out into East Harlem and the Bronx. The brothers tried their hand at several legitimate occupations and business ventures but ultimately turned their attention to counterfeiting. Yes, counterfeiting was a primary racket that led to the establishment of La Cosa Nostra in this country—perhaps not as sexy as Hollywood would like us to believe.

Giuseppe Morello took the reins as ringleader and developed great influence in the Corleone criminal communities of New York City. By the turn of the century, Morello had joined forces with Ignazio Lupo,[104] who had arrived in New York by 1899 to escape murder charges back in Sicily. Lupo married into the family on December 22, 1904, by taking Salvatrese Dora Terranova, Morello's stepsister, as his bride.

The core of Morello's small clan was Corleonisi, but other Italians were also attracted to the enigmatic leader—as were non-Italian criminals, perhaps impressed with his Mafia pedigree. Without the help of established criminal networks in this city, the Morellos may not have made the impact that they did.

On the morning of June 11, 1900, Giuseppe Morello and associate Colagero Meggiore were arrested and held on $5,000 bail, suspected by the Secret Service of producing counterfeit five-dollar bills. Four Irishmen, named Whalen, Green, Gleason and Thompson, were also picked up in the sweep, on suspicion of purchasing the crudely made currency for two dollars each and then distributing it in non-Italian Brooklyn and Queens communities. Morello, who gave his address as 337 East 106th Street, was held for about a week before being released due to lack of evidence.

The arrest did little to dissuade Morello from expanding his criminal enterprises over the next decade; however, the outfit would face a few obstacles along the way. In the fall of 1902, five members of Morello's ring were incarcerated for manufacturing counterfeit silver coins in a Hackensack, New Jersey home. Arrested during the sting was visiting Sicilian Mafia boss Vito Cascioferro, who gave his address as 361 First Avenue—he was ultimately released.

The fact that Cascioferro spent time in New York City with the Morello gang at the turn of the century does not mean that there was an official connection between the Sicilian and American Mafias, as is often implied. In fact, there is not much evidence to support that theory. Don Vito did work closely with the Morellos during his almost three years in America, but his activities in the United States are not known to have been on behalf of any Sicilian Mafia organization.

Giuseppe Morello was suspected in the July 1902 Brooklyn murder of Giuseppe Catania, thought to have had a falling out with the Morellos, but no charges were ever brought against the gang leader. Later that year, the small gang would take another hit when three of its members were again arrested in December for passing illegal currency through a Morristown, New Jersey bank.

After the 1902 counterfeiting arrests, the U.S. Secret Service kept a close eye on the Morellos. The homes and businesses of several gang members were under constant surveillance, especially Morello's "saloon and spaghetti kitchen" at 8 Prince Street, which served as the gang's headquarters.

That block of Prince Street between Bowery and Elizabeth would eventually become known to locals and authorities as "Black Hand Block." It was an epicenter of early Mafia activities in this city for close to two decades. The *New York Times* reported in 1911, "When detectives have wanted to get wind of an Italian criminal, they began their search at that address [8 Prince Street]."[105]

It was at 8 Prince Street where Vito Cascioferro held meetings with the Morellos during his time in America. It was also at the center of a sensational 1903 murder investigation, after the body of a Buffalo, New York man named Benedetto Madonia was found stuffed inside a sugar barrel on the sidewalk in front of 743 East Eleventh Street on the morning of Tuesday, April 14. (See Madonia, Benedetto, "Gangland Hits" chapter.)

After the "Barrel Murder," Giuseppe Morello moved the base of his operations from the Lower East to the Upper East Side. The gang leader set up a primitive printing press in an apartment at 329 East 106th Street, where he produced modest quantities of barely passable paper money.

8 Prince Street today. *Courtesy of Shirley Dluginski.*

Morello then sold these fake bills to Sicilian and Irish launderers (shovers) who purchased them at about forty cents on the dollar, redistributing them to saloons and gambling parlors across the five boroughs.

Beyond counterfeiting, Morello expanded into real estate and construction by establishing the Ignatz Florio Co-Operative Association Among Corleonesi in 1902. Company shares were offered to (and/or forced on) members of the Italian community, and Morello was soon handling property deals worth hundreds of thousands of dollars.

The Morellos flourished in the real estate market for a few years, both legitimately and otherwise, though the company folded by the end of the decade. By this time, the family's operations had branched out to Italian communities in major cities across the United States, like New Orleans, Buffalo, Philadelphia and Boston. They had accumulated enough money and power to pay off corrupt police and sway favor from local politicos. It appeared as though the Morellos were almost untouchable; however, the law finally caught up with the outfit by 1909.

In the summer of that year, Secret Service detectives secured a tenement apartment across the street from a Morello gang–run grocery at 235 East Ninety-seventh Street, which they suspected was operating as a front for the ring's counterfeiting racket. Throughout the fall of 1909, authorities recorded all the goings-on at that location and others and noticed a steady supply of inks and paper being shipped to a farm in Highland, New York, among other suspicious activities.

On November 15, 1909, authorities swept down on the store and made several arrests. Morello and Lupo were tracked down and arrested a few days later. The entire operation unraveled after the East Ninety-seventh Street raid and subsequent raids on gang member apartments, businesses and the upstate farmhouse where the fake bills were being produced. On February 19, 1910, Giuseppe Morello, Ignazio Lupo and six associates were convicted after a brief trial and sentenced to terms ranging from fifteen to thirty years.

When several attempts to free Giuseppe Morello over the next few years failed, Nicolo Terranova assumed control of the family. He held the position until 1916—when he was murdered during a war between the Corleones and their Neapolitan rivals, who began to muscle in on Sicilian territory, perhaps taking advantage of the fact that their feared leader was behind bars serving a thirty-year sentence.

The once mighty Morello outfit yielded to more powerful gangs for a few years until Giuseppe Masseria restored the family's position in the Italian underworld in the 1920s.

PETILLO, DAVID SILVIO

63 Mott Street, 1908; 15 Madison Street, 1930; 246 West Forty-eighth Street, 1958; 351 West Forty-second Street, 1960s; 30 Park Avenue, Apartment 16G, 1971

Alias: Little Davie, Anthony Ferrara, David Rosa, David Betillo, James J. Pilone

Born: March 20, 1908, New York City

Died: December 28, 1983, Spain (natural causes)

Association: Genovese crime family capo

With a criminal career spanning over half a century, Petillo is another relatively unknown yet influential Mafioso who is often overlooked in the history books. By the 1930s, "Little Davie" was one of the mob's most feared hit men, believed by authorities to have been Charlie Luciano's "number one agent." According to the FBI, as a contract killer, Petillo was involved in twenty to thirty murders in four cities by 1936—often with Petillo dressed as a woman.

The block where David Petillo grew up, Mott Street, circa 1900. *Library of Congress.*

David Petillo was born the fifth of six children to father Antonio Petillo, a street sweeper for the Department of Sanitation, and mother Michelina ("Maria") Loberti,[106] who arrived in New York City in 1885. He grew up at 63 Mott Street and occasionally attended PS 114 on James Street until officially dropping out at age fourteen.

While one of Petillo's brothers grew up to become an Italian police officer and another an IRS agent, young David was in and out of trouble from the time he was eleven, when he was first arrested for juvenile delinquency. At sixteen, Petillo spent his first term behind bars—sixty days for "jostling." Between 1931 and 1958, Petillo racked up at least nine adult convictions in New York City alone (under seven different aliases), for various offenses including armed robbery, compulsory prostitution, opium possession, larceny, extortion, racketeering, loan-sharking, gambling and murder. Between 1936 and 1972, Petillo would only enjoy about three years of freedom.

David Silvio Petillo was initiated into the Luciano (Genovese) organization by 1931 and, along with partner Charles "Chalutz" Gagliodoto, contracted to carry out murders for the bosses of the Detroit, Cleveland and Chicago Mafia organizations, including allegedly working for Al Capone in Chicago. It was during this time that "Little Davie" earned the reputation as the "cross-dressing killer," as he often dressed in drag in order to get close to unsuspecting victims.

Petillo had made a few trips to Italy in the early 1930s, accompanying Charlie Luciano on at least one voyage. Authorities considered Petillo to be Luciano's "right-hand man" by the time district attorney Thomas East Dewey had both men arrested on February 1, 1936. Witnesses claimed it was David Petillo who oversaw the $12-million-a-year alleged prostitution ring that led to the imprisonment and eventual deportation of Charlie "Lucky." It was said to be the largest sex trade operation in the country, with over three thousand prostitutes working at over two hundred brothels.

Supreme Court justice Philip McCook scolded Petillo during the sentencing, saying, "As Luciano's chief and most ruthless aide, you deserve no consideration from this court," before sentencing him to twenty-five to forty years behind bars.[107]

After two decades in Sing Sing prison, Petillo was paroled in April 1955 at age forty-eight. The game had changed during his years behind bars. His old friend Vito Genovese was on the verge of a hostile takeover of the family, and the main racket on the streets was narcotics. Petillo allegedly began trafficking heroin through various mob-backed after-hours clubs and bars but also became a member of the International Brotherhood of Teamsters, Chauffeurs and Warehouse Union Local 209—claiming to be employed at the William Abel Tailor Shop at 40 East Fifty-second Street for sixty-one dollars a week.

On June 29, 1958, Petillo was arrested for violating parole (a "misunderstanding") and was sent back to prison until 1967. By July of that year, Little Davie had moved into room 1805 of the Holland Hotel at 351 West Forty-second Street, where he was under constant surveillance by the FBI. In 1969, the feds even followed the ex-con on a trip to Italy, where the Petillo family owned an olive grove in Sierro di Acciaroli, Salerno.

Despite being pressed by authorities, Petillo became partners in several semi-legitimate after-hours nightclubs and adult cabarets, like the one he ran with Angelo Tuminaro at 11 East Sixteenth Street, where he spent most of his time. He also had an interest in one of the largest producers of hardcore porn at the time, called Arrow Film Labs, with its office at 75 Spring Street.

In 1971 or 1972, Petillo made capo and inherited the Genovese family's storied Little Italy crew, whose base of operations was a members-only club at 121 Mulberry Street. However, he suffered a heart attack and stroke soon after and went underground. The FBI lost contact with Petillo for a short time but found him in 1974 living in Brick Township, New Jersey (501 North Lake Shore Drive), in the house of Newark police chief Anthony Barres, who claimed he did not know about Petillo's criminal background.[108]

Believing the veteran gangster was in poor health, suffering from memory loss and retired from organized crime, authorities dropped their day-to-day surveillance of Petillo until 1981, when he was implicated in the February 1980 murder of ex–business partner Edward Vassallo (known as "Charles Talbot").

In October 1980, a mob informer agreed to wear a listening device, which helped the FBI record several conversations with Petillo over an eighteen-month period, ultimately leading to his indictment for the murder. However, before facing trial, Petillo fled to Mexico and eventually wound up in Malaga, Spain, where he died of natural causes in 1983 at the age of seventy-five, under the name James J. Pilone.

Polizzano, Ralph

36 East Fourth Street, Apartment 2, 1950s
Alias: n/a
Born: May 16, 1922, New York City
Died: [?]
Association: Genovese crime family

By the mid-1950s, Ralph Polizzano, brother Carmine and fellow mobsters Joseph Di Palermo, John Ormento and Natale Evola were allegedly organizing a multimillion-dollar international heroin-trafficking operation under Vito Genovese. The ring was based out of Ralph Polizzano's ground-floor apartment at 36 East Fourth Street, which was where the crew was said to "cut" and package heroin imported from Cuba, Mexico and Puerto Rico for street distribution in North America.

36 East Fourth Street, the site of Ralph Polizzano's apartment and alleged narcotics plant, today.

When a distributor for the ring named Salvatore Marino was busted in July 1957, he confessed to couriering drugs for the outfit and gave up the names and addresses of his contacts. When Polizzano was arrested, the gangster chose to cooperate after a rough interrogation and led narcotics detectives to a stash of heroin and cocaine above his kitchen cabinet, as well as to equipment used for weighing and packaging in a separate room.

During the trial, several witnesses corroborated Marino's story. One man named Nelson Silva Cantellops testified that he witnessed Ralph Polizzano diluting the drugs himself and was paid directly by the Polizzano brothers on several occasions to transport packages throughout the United States. In one case, he alleged that he picked up a suitcase from Carmine Polizzano in Key West, Florida, and delivered it via train to Ralph Polizzano (on East Fourth Street), who in turn paid him $600 (and tipped him an ounce of heroin).[109]

Polizzano petitioned for a mistrial on the grounds that certain evidence was coerced, but the judge did not buy it—he was sentenced to fifteen years in prison.

PRESINZANO, FRANK

236 Cherry Street, 1920; 167 Mott Street, 1950s
Alias: Pardini
Born: August 2, 1902, New York City
Died: [?]
Association: Bonanno crime family

Though his official title of employment was "fish loader," the five-foot, three-inch Presinzano was a highly regarded Mafioso who used violence and intimidation as a "boss" of the Fulton Fish Market racket.

Frank was the first of six children born to immigrant parents Salvatore and Rosa Presinzano. In a 1920 census, eighteen-year-old Frank is listed as being in the "trucking business"; however, by that time, he had already run into trouble with the law and was charged as an adult.

Between 1919 and the 1950s, Presinzano was arrested for a variety of infractions, from assault and robbery to weapons violations and petty larceny.

By the 1950s, he was suspected of engaging in heroin trafficking with his brother Angelo Presinzano and Carmine Galante, and he had at least one narcotics-related conviction during that time.

QUARTIERO, LAWRENCE

145 West End Avenue, 1920; 410 West Fifty-fourth Street, 1950s
Alias: Larry
Born: May 24, 1923, New York City
Died: [?]
Association: Genovese and Lucchese crime families

Quartiero was an influential West Side racketeer, convicted narcotics trafficker and, according to the FBN, an "expert jewelery and fur thief and fence."

Born to Michael Quartiero, a laborer, and Restitula (Rosetta) Catugna, young Larry's first arrest came in 1940, at age seventeen. Following was a string of arrests—including felonious assault, gambling, burglary and petty larceny—spanning four decades.

As early as 1949, Larry Quartiero was allegedly involved in large-scale narcotics trafficking. On April 23, 1956, he was sentenced to five years in prison for his role in a ring that included Joe Valachi. The ring was said to smuggle large quantities of heroin by boat from France, Italy and South America. His co-conspirator, Lucchese gang member Giacomo Reina, son of former family boss Gaetano Reina, was also sent to prison, along with two others, but somehow Valachi's conviction was reversed in 1957.[110]

After prison, Quartiero continued to build his influence in the union rackets of the shipping yards and warehouses along the West Side of Manhattan, but he pretty much stayed under the radar until 1983, when the sixty-year-old was arrested, along with three others, for a scheme to fix races at Roosevelt and Yonkers racetracks by drugging certain horses and betting against them. A horse groomer named James Veno assisted in the ring.

Larry Quartiero was convicted on RICO charges in April 1983, receiving a one-year prison sentence and five years' probation. However, a federal appeals court dismissed the charges in October 1983, blaming "overzealous prosecutors" for "misusing the system."[111]

RAO, JOSEPH

453 114th Street, 1920; 413 East 117th Street, 1930; 337 East 116th Street, 1950s
Alias: Joey, Joseph Cangro, Cangero
Born: March 12, 1901, New York City
Died: May 10, 1962, New York City (stroke)
Association: Luciano/Genovese crime family

This veteran gangster is rarely written about these days, but he was one of the twentieth century's most influential and visible mobsters. Joey Rao earned his criminal stripes as one of the earliest and most dedicated members of the murderous Dutch Schultz gang, before joining his brother-in-law (and sometimes partner in crime) Joseph "Stretch" Stacci in the Luciano (Genovese) family.

Rao grew up in East Harlem with his widowed mother, Frances, who immigrated to New York from Italy in 1883. He married his wife, Lena, in 1923 and had two children with her by 1930 while living at 413 East 117th Street.

Joey Rao mug shots.

With a record dating back to 1920, this Harlem gangster's criminal career was a long and rocky one. His dedication to Dutch Schultz nearly got him killed in a 1931 bootlegging war with Vincent "Mad Dog" Coll, a former Schultz enforcer who branched out with his own gang. On July 28, 1931, Rao survived a brazen summer's eve hit outside the crew's Helmar Social Club at 208 East 107th Street. Six men with shotguns and automatic weapons fired more than sixty shots from a speeding automobile. The assassins missed their target, but five children were hit in the attack, one of whom died.

To give an idea of the sentiment toward Italians in the slums at the time, the following is a passage from *Time* magazine regarding the shooting:

> *Life in 107th Street reaches its noisiest, most ebullient phase after the dinner hour. Fat, oily women, some without shoes, rattle dirty dishes. Their men sit smoking in front of the Helmar Social Club. Their litters of children play and quarrel shrilly all through the street. Into this babble and filth and smell one evening last week came Terror.*[112]

The courtyards behind East 107th Street, facing east from Third Avenue, in 1900. *Library of Congress.*

While serving a two-year term on Welfare Island Penitentiary for assault and conspiracy in the early 1930s, five-foot-seven, two-hundred-pound Rao was one of three "prison bosses," running a gang that organized a narcotics and gambling operation and sold special privileges to other inmates. During his stay, Rao famously raised pigeons and lived in the spacious hospital ward, to which he referred as "politicians' flats," where he made homemade beer, held parties, kept a personal radio and had iceboxes full of snacks and non-prison-issued delicacies. (A 1939 Warner Brothers film starring John Garfield, entitled *Blackwell's Island*, roughly fictionalizes Rao's pampered prison life during this time.)

A row between Rao's followers and a rival gang led to a riot and the death of one inmate in 1932, prompting a raid on the prison and a shake-up in the administration. The prison would close for good after 110 years in 1936, when a new city prison was built on Riker's Island, which is still in operation.

In January 1935, with just a month left on his sentence, Rao was convicted on a two-year-old charge for the assault of a police officer outside an East Harlem dancehall on January 4, 1932, and sentenced to two years in Sing Sing, a term he served immediately after being released from Welfare Island.

In April 1939, Rao, Joseph Stacci and two others were arrested for vagrancy in a restaurant at 2246 First Avenue, but charges were almost immediately dismissed. Another vagrancy charge failed to stick in 1943.

In 1946, Rao and Michael "Trigger Mike" Coppola were implicated in the election day murder of Joseph Scottoriggio, a Republican party district captain who was viciously clubbed and stomped to death in front of his wife on the way to an East Harlem polling station. The men were held without bail for over a year as material witnesses, but neither was convicted.

By the 1950s, Rao was, according to the FBN, the "undisputed boss of all [heroin] rackets in the area of 1st Avenue and East 116th Street." He was also the top man in Anthony Strollo's crew and was instrumental in expanding the family's racketeering operation into the shipping ports and terminals of New Jersey.

In May 1950, Joey Rao was listed by the Justice Department as being among the "top 150 racketeers" in the country, in the company of mob heavyweights like Frank Costello, Joe Adonis, Ralph Capone, Mickey Cohen and Meyer Lansky.[113] During the 1952 Crime Commission Hearings, several witnesses, including Gaetano Lucchese, were questioned about their relationship with Joseph Rao.

RAO, VINCENT

161 East 108ᵗʰ Street, 1910; 235 East 107ᵗʰ Street, 1930s
Alias: n/a
Born: June 21, 1898, Palermo, Sicily (b. Rao, Vincenzo Giovanni)
Died: September 25, 1988, Florida
Association: Lucchese crime family consigliere

Vincent Rao, not related to Joseph, was born in Palermo to Antonio Rao and Liboria Colletti before moving with his family to East Harlem in 1899. Rao's father is listed in a 1910 census report as a laborer, and older sister Mary is listed as a cigar maker.

Vincent's older brother, Calogero "Charles" Rao (born January 2, 1889), joined him in several semi-legitimate business ventures, making a fortune in the construction industry by the 1930s —specifically, in lathing, hoisting and plastering. The brothers owned their own construction businesses and held stock in several others. Calogero replaced Anthony "Little Augie" Carfano as head of the mob-backed Ace Lathing Company after the gangster was shot to death on a Queens street in 1959.

Vincent Rao was also a real estate investor, owning several East Harlem properties, including his home at 235 East 107ᵗʰ Street, where Joe Valachi and two other gunmen assassinated a man named Stefano "Steve" Rannelli on November 19, 1936.

Joe Valachi later claimed that Rao was a member of the Mafia Commission.

235 East 107ᵗʰ Street, 1912. *Library of Congress.*

RUGGIERO, BENJAMIN

125 Oliver Street, 1930; 10 Monroe Street
Alias: Lefty Guns, Lefty Two-Guns
Born: April 19, 1926, New York City
Died: November 24, 1994, New York City
Association: Bonanno crime family

Benjamin Ruggiero is probably best known for unknowingly sponsoring undercover detective Joseph Pistone into the Mafia, as portrayed by Al Pacino in the movie *Donnie Brasco*.

"Lefty Two Guns" was born to Fiori and Frances Ruggiero in the Fourth Ward neighborhood of the Lower East Side, where he formed early relationships with fellow future mobsters like Anthony Mirra. Both were initiated into the Bonanno organization about the same time (by the 1950s) and would serve in the same crew throughout their lives.

Over the following couple of decades, Ruggiero staked out slivers of several small fencing, bookmaking and loan-sharking operations and invested in a handful of semi-legitimate businesses.

Insiders remember "Benny" (which his family and neighbors called him) as being a simple and generally affable man. He wasn't a "what are you looking at?" kind of guy, and he didn't have grandiose ambitions of taking over La Cosa Nostra. Ruggiero was said to be a loyal and enthusiastic wise guy but was content with his position in the pecking order and managed to remain below the radar throughout most of his criminal career.

That all changed the day Anthony Mirra introduced him to "Donnie Brasco" in the 1970s. The supposed jewel thief and the aloof gangster hit it off. Ruggiero never suspected Brasco to be an undercover FBI agent named Joseph Pistone. The oversight ended up leading to dozens of convictions and the murders of Anthony Mirra and Dominick "Sonny Black" Napolitano, Bonanno members who initially introduced Brasco to the family.

In the 1997 film *Donnie Brasco*, based on Pistone's 1987 book, *Donnie Brasco: My Undercover Life in the Mafia*, the viewer is left with the impression that Ruggiero was killed in retribution, but that is not the case. The sixty-eight-year-old succumbed to lung cancer just three years before the movie was released.

When I asked a neighborhood old-timer how well Pacino captured the gangster's personalty, he replied, "Acceptable."

SALERNO, ANTHONY MICHAEL

344 East 116ᵗʰ Street, 1950s
Alias: Fat Tony, Punchy
Born: August 5, 1913, New York City
Died: July 27, 1992, Springfield, Missouri
Association: Luciano/Genovese crime family front boss

With a criminal record dating back to 1932, East Harlem native Anthony Salerno was a respected veteran mobster who got his start just as Prohibition came to an end, working for the Charlie Luciano family's uptown crew led by "Trigger Mike" Coppola.

Earning the reputation as an intelligent and trustworthy associate, Salerno gained more and more responsibility through the decades, becoming one of the Genovese family's most successful leaders of all time. The low-profile mob boss not only generated an enormous amount of money for the organization, but he also had a knack for counseling disgruntled underlings, settling disputes, averting unnecessary wars and avoiding prison (at least until the end of his career).

Just because Salerno chose to stay out of the spotlight does not mean he did not get around. According to author John L. Smith, the mob boss was good friends with entertainer Frank Sinatra. In his book *Running Scared: The Life and Treacherous Times of Las Vegas Casino King Steve Wynn*, Smith reports a story told to the FBI about how Salerno convinced casino mogul Steve Wynn to hire Sinatra as his Golden Nugget casino spokesman. As a result, profits rose dramatically, and Salerno was able to install mob associates into key positions at Wynn's Atlantic City and Vegas casinos.

Salerno was elevated to the position of Genovese family front boss in 1981, replacing Brooklyn-based Alphonse Frank "Funzi" Tieri, who passed away in March of that year. Though according to many Mafia insiders, including Salerno's one-time confidant turned informant Anthony "Fish" Cafaro, the real boss of the family was Philip "Benny Squint" Lombardo, who took over the outfit upon the death of Vito Genovese in 1969. Lombardo was allegedly grooming Vincent Gigante for the position (which he secured in the 1980s), using several perceived bosses like Salerno in the process to steer attention away from both himself and Gigante.

Salerno's reign as front boss did not last long. The FBI bugged his longtime headquarters at the Palma Boys Social Club on 115th Street in the early 1980s, leading to a one-hundred-year prison sentence on RICO charges in 1986. In 1988, Salerno was awarded another seventy-year sentence for his role in a high-rise construction bid-rigging scheme.

The seasoned mob boss died of a stroke inside a Springfield, Missouri federal prison hospital at age eighty.

SIANO, FIORE

2281 First Avenue, 1954
Alias: Fiore Sanguino, Fury
Born: June 22, 1927, New York City
Died: 1964? (disappeared)
Association: Genovese crime family

Siano was the nephew of infamous mob informer Joe Valachi and alleged major narcotics supplier to local black street gangs. He was described by assistant United States attorney Fred Nathan in 1954 as the "principal dealer in cocaine along the Eastern seaboard."[114]

The first arrest for Siano came in 1948 on burglary charges. He was recruited into organized crime through his uncle Joe Valachi, who helped set up Fiore in the illegal narcotics trade in the East Harlem area. Soon, Siano was allegedly carrying out hits for the Genovese crime family, making his bones with the September 20, 1952 murder of Lucchese soldier turned informer Eugenio "Gene" Giannini.

Siano was said to have been recruited again for the 1953 assassination of Steven Franse, a mob associate and longtime close friend of both Vito Genovese and Joe Valachi.

As the gangland legend goes, Genovese left Franse in charge of keeping an eye on his wife, Anna, who was in the process of divorcing Vito and threatening to go public about her husband's methods of income. Supposedly, Genovese further suspected Anna of carrying on affairs with both men and women under Franse's nose, an especially humiliating situation for the rising Mafia boss—so appropriate action had to be taken to save face. As the story goes, Genovese couldn't bring himself to harm Anna, so despite three decades of trusting friendship, he ordered Franse killed. The contract again went to Joe Valachi and his crew of young hit men.

On the morning of June 19, 1953, the body of Steven Franse was found in the rear seat of his car, which was parked in front of 164 East Thirty-seventh Street. Just hours earlier, he had allegedly been lured to a restaurant by old friend Valachi and then jumped by Fiore Siano and Pasquale Pagano, beaten and strangled to death with a chain.

Siano was not convicted for either murder, but he was sentenced to eight years in federal prison on November 27, 1954, after pleading guilty to selling "the highest quality of cocaine at $1,500 an ounce."

The last anyone ever saw of Fiore Siano was in early May 1964, when he was allegedly led out of Patsy's Pizzeria at 2287 First Avenue with three unidentified men.

SORGE, SANTO

222 East Fifty-seventh Street
Alias: n/a
Born: January 11, 1908, Caltanissetta, Sicily
Died: May 1972, New York City
Association: Bonanno crime family

Considered one of the "great unknowns" of the American Mafia, Sorge was one of the most powerful Mafioso in the United States who also wielded great political power back in Italy. He was a good friend to Charlie Luciano and was thought of as an important liaison between the U.S. and Italian Mafias.

In May 1948, about thirty Sicilians were smuggled into the country via the Port of Philadelphia aboard the SS *Panormus*. Many of the aliens were carrying "substantial quantities" of heroin, which they agreed to transport in exchange for being brought to the United States. The FBN determined that Carlo Gambino was involved in the operation, as was a "representative of" the Santo Sorge Trading Company, located at 196 First Avenue.

Shortly before the Apalachin Meeting of 1957, Sorge, Joe Bonanno and Carmine Galante visited Palermo for a meeting with Charlie Luciano,[115] many believe in order to receive input from Luciano regarding matters of the upcoming conference.

In the late 1960s, the FBI named Sorge as one of the possible successors to Gaspare DiGregorio during the Bonanno family upheaval.

In Palermo during the spring of 1968, Sorge was one of seventeen high-profile U.S. and Italian Mafioso facing up to fifteen years in an Italian prison on charges of operating an international narcotics and currency trafficking ring.[116] Dubbed the "patriarchs of the Cosa Nostra," codefendants included ten top Sicilian Mafioso, like Giuseppe Genco Russo, and seven American crime bosses, including Joe Bonanno and Carmine Galante from New York, Rafaele Quarasano of Detroit and Francesco Scimone of Boston.

Before the historic trial started, Judge Aldo Vigneri made an unprecedented trip to the United States in order to interview U.S. law enforcement officials and visit Mafia turncoat Joe Valachi—on whose testimony the prosecutors' case was largely based.

The trial began on March 14, 1968, in Palermo, Sicily, and was presided over by three judges with no jury. At the preliminary hearing, Sorge's attorneys moved to dismiss the indictment on the grounds that his client, who remained in the United States, was not advised of the charges against him. After two hours of deliberation, the motion was denied. Lawyers then requested permission to subpoena former partner Joe Valachi and New York City police officers Ralph Salerno and John Shanley. The court agreed, provided Sorge pay for all expenses. The witnesses were scheduled to appear in Palermo on April 30; however, they never made the trip.

By May, defense lawyers had cross-examined several witnesses, trying to establish Sorge's credibility as a legitimate businessman. On May 7 and 8, several people took the stand and testified that Sorge was head of a legitimate Sicilian company called Mediterranea Metals. On June 25, Sorge and all codefendants were acquitted.

Four years later, Sorge died of natural causes at the age of sixty-four.

SPECIALE, SALVATORE

209 East 107th Street, 1930; 213 East 107th Street, 1950s
Alias: Benny, Sal the Beak
Born: March 12, 1916, New York City
Died: March 25, 1996, Centereach, New York
Association: Lucchese crime family

This stocky, five-foot-three, 170-pound gangster was a trusted associate of the Mafia's top bosses and said to have had a large controlling interest in East Harlem's illegal lottery and gambling operations.

Salvatore was born in East Harlem to Francesco Paolo Speciale, who is listed in a 1930 census as a laundry factory driver, and Marietta Rao, the sister of mobster Vincent Rao. They were married at Mount Carmel Church (447 East 115th Street) in November 1910.

East 107th Street, between Second and Third Avenue, in 1912. These buildings no longer exist. Two full blocks of East 107th Street, between Third and First Avenues, have been cleared to make way for an apartment complex. *Library of Congress.*

Salvatore's first of several arrests came in 1934, at age eighteen. Over the following decades, "Sal the Beak" accumulated an impressive criminal record, including convictions for vagrancy, bookmaking, grand larceny, gambling and narcotics violations.

STOPPELLI, JOHN

143 Thompson Street, 1910; 153 Madison Street, 1950s; 200 East Thirty-sixth Street, 1977

Alias: John the Bug

Born: April 10, 1907, New York City (b. Stoppelli, Innocenzio)

Died: January 10, 1993, New York City

Association: Genovese crime family

By the 1950s, according to the FBN, Stoppelli was a "trusted inner-circle Mafia leader" and "one of the most active large-scale, wholesale narcotic traffickers in the United States," working for the Lower Manhattan crew of the Genovese crime family led by Anthony Strollo.

"John the Bug" was born in Little Italy to Rocco Stoppelli, an electrician, and Carmela Miraglio, a cigar store worker, Italian immigrants who were married in New York City in 1900. As a teen, John Stoppelli formed a local stickup and robbery crew, admitting to police during a 1926 arrest that he lived off the "profits of hold-ups."[117]

In March 1926, while living with his family at 926 East 216th Street in the Bronx, nineteen-year-old John Stoppelli was arrested for the October 1925 murder of Louis Bernardo in a pool hall at 108 Thompson Street. Stoppelli's partner, Peter Cinnamo, admitted to killing Bernardo in a fight and was sentenced for homicide. Stoppelli was charged with burglary.

On April 19, 1938, at 2:15 a.m., a beautiful professional dancer named Thelma Giroux fell naked to her death from the fifth floor of the former Hotel Lincoln at Eighth Avenue and West Forty-fifth Street. When police went to the woman's room to investigate, they found Stoppelli, who had been dating Giroux for two years. After a few hours of questioning, the known gangster was released, claiming that Giroux had committed suicide.

The rear of the tenement at 134 Thompson Street in 1912, across the street from where John Stoppelli was raised. *National Child Labor Committee Collection, Library of Congress.*

Stoppelli told police that the couple had just returned to the hotel after a night on the town, and out of nowhere, Giroux had stated, "I'm sick and tired of it all. Goodbye. So long. It's all over."[118] Stoppelli then claimed he stepped out of the room for a moment and upon returning found Giroux missing and the window open. The authorities bought the story, and Stoppelli was released.

It was the second such mysterious death in less than a week. A twenty-two-year-old woman named Norma DeMarco had "committed suicide" by jumping out of a twelfth-story window at 138 West Fifty-eighth Street on April 14, just two days after witnessing the shooting of police officer Humbert Maruzzi during a holdup at the Howdy Club, at 47 West Third Street. DeMarco was credited with saving the officer's life. When a gunman was preparing to shoot the wounded cop in the back, DeMarco screamed, and the shot missed. The brave heroine was then pistol-whipped while attempting to wrestle the gun away from the thug and still had bandages on her head the night she died. Police lieutenant Thomas Martin ruled that a "sudden mental aberration" caused DeMarco to jump.[119]

On August 8, 1949, John the Bug was sentenced to six years in prison based on the testimony of a fingerprint expert, who claimed to have lifted a partial print of Stoppelli's ring finger from an envelope of heroin confiscated during an Oakland, California hotel room raid. The only problem was that Stoppelli had proof that he was three thousand miles away in New York City, where he checked in with a parole officer.

Despite contradicting evidence, Stoppelli was convicted. In November 1951, the FBI examined the print in question and concluded that it was not Stoppelli's. President Harry S Truman ordered that "the Bug" be released.

In January 1977, Stoppelli was rounded up with Genovese capo James Napoli and held on charges of conspiracy and promoting gambling. The ring was busted when an undercover officer using the name "Joseph DeVito" infiltrated the group in 1974 and worked for two years as a "pick-up man" (someone who collects and delivers gambling records for "district managers" or "controllers"). Stoppelli and Napoli were said to be partners in the multimillion-dollar operation.

Stoppelli died of natural causes at eighty-six years old, ending a sixty-plus-year career in crime.

STROLLO, ANTHONY

177 Thompson Street, 1920
Alias: Tony Bender
Born: June 18, 1899, New York City
Died: April 8, 1962(?), Fort Lee, New Jersey (disappeared)
Association: Genovese crime family acting boss

Anthony Strollo was born to forty-four-year-old Leone Strollo and thirty-two-year-old Giovannina "Jennie" Nigro, Calabrian immigrants who arrived in New York City in the late 1880s. He grew up at this address on the outskirts of Little Italy (coincidentally, the same building where Vincent Gigante was born in 1928), where his father owned a local candy store.

Strollo's arrest record dates back to 1926, when the young gangster lent his criminal talents to the Masseria crime family before wisely defecting, along with Charlie Luciano, Vito Genovese and others, to Salvatore Maranzano's Brooklyn-based clan in 1930 during the Castellammarese War.

When the Mafia was restructured in 1931, Strollo's allegiances paid off, and he was recruited into the Luciano (Genovese) crime family, where he took over operations of the organization's Little Italy crew by 1935. Strollo was said to be one of the few good friends that Vito Genovese had. The pair participated in a double wedding ceremony in March 1934 and stayed close for the next couple of decades.

By the 1950s, Strollo was allegedly controlling much of the Genovese family nightclub, waterfront and policy racket operations, which extended into northern New Jersey. At about midnight on March 14, 1952, Jersey City mayor John V. Kenny was observed meeting with Strollo for ninety-seven minutes at the Warwick Hotel (65 West Fifty-fourth Street), for which the politician was questioned for three hours by the State Crime Commission on May 27. Mayor Kenny first denied everything but eventually admitted to meeting with the known mobster in "an attempt to end waterfront unrest."[120]

It was speculated that the New York mob's infiltration of the docks in Mayor Kenney's district upset the politico's New Jersey mob associates, who put pressure on him to do something about the situation. When Strollo offered to "help," a meeting was set up by a mutual associate, entertainer Phil Regan, who hosted the event at his Midtown hotel suite.

In the end, Mayor Kenny caved in to Strollo, action that apparently did not please his constituents. Anthony Strollo's brother, Dominick, who helped oversee the waterfront operations, was found beaten and unconscious on a Jersey City pier on July 5.

On April 1, 1953, it was uncovered that fifty-six longshoreman, who got their jobs because of Mayor Kenny's influence, had criminal records. Most of them worked at the Army Claremont Terminal—which the military abandoned in November 1952 because racketeering made it too costly to operate—the same location where Dominick Strollo was found beaten.

According to Joe Valachi, Anthony Strollo was his first boss when initiated into the Luciano family in the early 1930s. Valachi also testified that Vito Genovese was behind Strollo's 1962 disappearance. In a televised 1963 hearing, Valachi told the world that upon hearing news reports of Strollo's disappearance, Genovese stated that it was "the best thing that should happen."[121]

In 1972, FBI surveillance picked up a conversation in which Jersey mobster Ruggiero "Richie the Boot" Boiardo claimed responsibility for the murder of Strollo, though feds believed it might have been an intentional ploy to mislead them.

Many insiders believe Genovese had longtime friend Strollo murdered because he disobeyed orders to not sell drugs. Others have since claimed that the mobster faked his own death and lived out the rest of his life in Florida. The world may never know. The body of Anthony Strollo has never been found, and the disappearance remains officially unsolved.

TOURINE, CHARLES, SR.

40 Central Park South, 1940s–1970s
Alias: Charlie the Blade
Born: March 26, 1906, New Jersey
Died: May 28, 1980, Miami, Florida
Association: Luciano/Genovese crime family capo

This Jersey-born mob heavyweight was a big-time gambler with interests in New York, New Jersey, Las Vegas, Miami and Cuba. He was said to have been considered for the boss position when Vito Genovese passed away in 1969; however, sources say that the fact that he was illiterate prevented the move.

Born to two recent Italian immigrants, Frank, a retail clerk, and mother Mary, young Charles Tourine grew up at 68 Main Street in Matawan, New Jersey. Tourine began his mob career working with a Jersey-based Luciano/Genovese crew led by Richard Bioardo.

On December 15, 1944, thirteen members of an alcohol-manufacturing ring were sentenced to a total of thirty-five years in prison after pleading guilty to running four illegal alcohol stills in Union Township, New Jersey. Tourine, who was living at the swanky San Moritz Hotel at 40 Central Park West, allegedly headed the operation and was sentenced to five years behind bars.

In 1951, Tourine was included on a government list of 126 notorious underworld figures whose income taxes were being investigated.[122]

Profiles

On April 29, 1968, New York customs agents uncovered a bundle of illegal pornographic magazines in a crate shipped from Copenhagen. The contraband was eventually traced to Tourine, who was indicted on May 21, 1969, for conspiring to bribe customs agents in order to smuggle $250,000 worth of adult literature into the country. During the October 1970 trial, all witnesses refused to answer questions, and no convictions were awarded.

In January 1970, while investigating the relationship between the motion picture industry and organized crime, the Joint Legislative Committee on Crime played a tape of a conversation between Tourine and a man named Kirk Kerkorian, controlling stockholder of Metro-Goldwyn-Mayer studios and founding partner of the original MGM Hotel in Las Vegas. In the 1961 recording, Tourine explained to Kirkorian the best way to send him $21,300. A check was to be given to movie star George Raft—the native New York actor famous for playing mobsters on the big screen—who was to cash the check and deliver it to Tourine. Of course, all parties refused to answer questions, and no explanation was ever made as to what the $21,300 was for.

In November 1970, Tourine was spotted having lunch three times with Frank Costello at Gatsby's Restaurant, at 20 East Forty-first Street. These meetings, held just months after the death of Vito Genovese, led authorities to speculate that Costello was coaxed out of retirement to help sort out the family's transition.

The semi-retired Charles Tourine had moved to Miami, Florida, by 1976 but never turned down a good business opportunity. In August of that year, Tourine pleaded innocent to federal charges stemming from a scheme to establish a gambling and prostitution ring along the new Alaskan pipeline. After a lengthy trial, Tourine and five co-conspirators were acquitted by October 1977.

On February 26, 1977, Tourine was one of five high-level mobsters, including Meyer Lansky, to be subpoenaed by the Dade County state attorney's office to answer questions about the May 1976 murder of a former Mafioso named John Rosselli, whose body was found stuffed in an oil drum in Biscayne Bay, Florida. Rosselli had testified before several grand juries and committees about an alleged plot by the CIA to kill Fidel Castro by recruiting the Mafia.

Tourine's son, Charles Jr. (later known as Charles Del Monico), followed in his father's footsteps and racked up quite a criminal career himself. He was also born in New Jersey but was living at 420 East Sixty-fourth Street by the 1960s.

Tramaglino, Victor

302 East Twelfth Street, 1912; 214 First Avenue, 1932
Alias: Victor Romano
Born: March 19, 1912, New York City (b. Tramaglino, Vittorio)
Died: May 26, 1980
Association: Genovese crime family soldier

Born to Lorenzo and Amolia Tramaglino in an apartment above John's Restaurant at 302 East Twelfth Street, the future Genovese soldier attended local PS 19 (the same school Charlie Luciano attended), where the bright student excelled academically and was allowed to skip two grades.

Lorenzo Tramaglino, an insurance salesman, fought hard to keep his eight sons out of trouble; one time he actually turned one of Victor's brothers in to police when he was caught gambling in the street. Despite Lorenzo's efforts, the influence of older neighborhood hoodlums like Joseph Biondo set Victor up for a life of crime. In fact, his neighbors at the time read like a who's who of aspiring mobsters: Joe N. Gallo (future Gambino consigliere), George "Lefty "Rizzo, Billy and Tony Esposito, Thomas "Bullets" Licatta (Tramaglino's future boss) and Matteo "Marty" DeLorenzo, the future Genovese capo who made headlines in the 1970s for his role in the Vatican Connection.

Victor Tamaglino's first arrest came at age eleven, when he was collared with two other kids for a petty theft five days before Christmas 1923. They were caught attempting to steal a toy from a display rack at a local shop. Spending most of his childhood in and out of reform schools and detention centers for truancy, Tramaglino formed a lifelong relationship at a young age with many of the men he would work with throughout his life.

Matteo DeLorenzo was with Tramaglino during an early arrest on March 20, 1932. In that incident, the pair attempted to rob a Greek bookmaker named Sempros, who was making his collection rounds on East Fourteenth Street. A man called "Pepe" was recruited as a lookout.

Tramaglino followed the bookie into an East Fourteenth Street apartment building hallway while DeLorenzo stood guard across the street. When a suspicious beat cop happened upon the scene, Pepe, who was a few doors away, fled without warning his accomplices.

The officer followed Tramaglino into the building, gun drawn. The armed gangster swung around and came face to face with the barrel of a police revolver. In the heat of the moment, the two exchanged shots, and Tramaglino was struck in the side of his head and shoulder. When he tried to run, a second officer shot him in the knee.

DeLorenzo was picked up across the street, and Pepe got away. As was customary of the "code," the lowest man on the totem pole was usually required to take the fall, and Tramaglino faced twenty-five years for attempted murder alone, plus additional gun charges. DeLorenzo walked away with a two-year sentence.

Instead of facing a jury, Tramaglino opted for a twenty-year plea deal and was sent to Sing Sing. As chance would have it, while Tramaglino was serving time, Pepe showed up in the same prison on an unrelated charge. He was stabbed to death soon after being admitted. No charges were ever filed, but authorities suspected Tramaglino and transferred him to Attica, where he finished his sentence.

By the time Tramaglino was released in 1946, DeLorenzo was already made, and he helped Tramaglino join the Mafia. He didn't forget that Tramaglino took the rap in 1932 and served his twenty years quietly (he didn't rat anybody out—a sure sign of loyalty).

Tramaglino was recruited into the Genovese organization that year, and his first boss was Thomas "Bullets" Licatta, whose crew operated out of the same Lower East Side neighborhood—the East Village—where they grew up. Licatta and Tramaglino were close—"Bullets" was even best man at Tramaglino's wedding.

When Thomas Licatta died in 1952, Cosmo "Gus" Frasca took over the Genovese family's East Village crew. From that point on, Tramaglino stayed out of narcotics and focused on loan-sharking and gambling. By the 1960s, he was running some of the biggest games in the city, essentially floating underground casinos in makeshift apartments, hotel rooms and café cellars.

On February 5, 1963, the FBI released an internal memo that listed 347 suspected Mafia members operating in New York City, requesting that individual investigations be conducted on each. Victor Tramaglino and his brother Julio were listed alongside fellow mobsters Frank Mari, Ralph Polizzano and Carmine "Sonny Pinto" Di Biase, a close friend of Victor Tramaglino and future accused assassin of "Crazy Joe" Gallo.

WANTED FOR MURDER

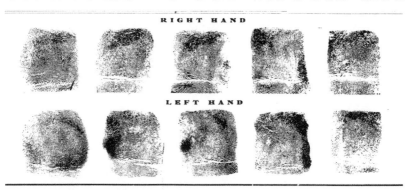

RIGHT HAND

LEFT HAND

DESCRIPTION—Age, 36 years; height, 5 feet, 7½ inches; weight, 150 pounds; brown eyes; dark chestnut hair; fair complexion; small scar on left temple at end of eyebrow. Last known address 1318 71st Street, Brooklyn, N. Y. Photo Number in New York Gallery, B-82088.

This Department holds an indictment warrant charging Frasca with the shooting and killing of one Ferdinand Boccia, at No. 533 Metropolitan Ave., Brooklyn, N. Y., on September 19, 1934.

Kindly search your Prison Records as this man may be serving a sentence for some minor offense.

If located, arrest, and hold as a fugitive from justice, and advise DETECTIVE DIVISION, by wire.

LEWIS J. VALENTINE, Police Commissioner
TELEPHONE: SPring 7-3100

GUS FRASCA alias COSMO FRASCA

Cosmo "Gus" Fracsa, wanted for the murder of Ferdinand Boccia in 1934. *NYPD, New York City Municipal Archives.*

Victor Tramaglino was also said to be close with 1970s front boss Alphonse Frank "Funzi" Tieri, who, when still just a soldier in the late 1940s, fell ill and required medical attention. While in the hospital, Tramaglino went out of his way to ensure collections were made on behalf of his fellow gangster. Tieri would never forget that and always looked out for him.

Tramaglino was busted one last time in 1969, for running an enormously successful gambling operation out of a building at 209 West Seventy-ninth Street with partners Sonny Pinto, Hugh Mulligan (Irish), Charlie Blum (Jewish), Stanley Ackerman (Jewish) and "Spanish" Ray Marquez (Hispanic). It was allegedly Marquez's influence that made the venue so successful because he brought in Puerto Rican gamblers from uptown who "loved to spend money," according to one source.

Ailing sixty-eight-year-old Victor Tramaglino died of a heart attack on May 26, 1980, while on his first vacation from the city in over thirty years.

TUMINARO, ANGELO

38 Hamilton Street, 1917; 152 Madison Street, 1920; 234 Cherry Street, 1930; 110 Henry Street, 1934; 24 Rutgers Street, 1950s

Alias: Tumensio, Little Angie

Born: February 22, 1910, New York City[123] (b. Tumminaro, Angelo)

Died: [?]

Association: Lucchese crime family

This five-foot-two, 135-pound gangster was the second of thirteen children born to Pasquale "Patchy" Tuminaro and Maria "Mary" Venera Presinzano, Sicilian immigrants who married in New York City in 1904. "Patchy" is listed in documents as a laborer, longshoreman and Department of Sanitation worker. One of Angelo's younger brothers (by nineteen years), Frank, would follow Angelo into organized crime.

"Little Angie" had a record dating back to 1929. He was married to a woman named Bella Stein, said to be the daughter of an influential Jewish racketeer. This relationship made Tuminaro an important liaison between Italian and Jewish criminal networks.

In November 1934, twenty-three-year-old Tuminaro was arrested, along with Frank Lisi and two other men, for holding up a restaurant at 36 Peck Slip on April 7. They made off with $1,200. That arrest came immediately after charges of vagrancy against the men were dropped following a New York City police commissioner's pre-election order to round up known thugs in order to curb voter fraud at the polls. Though the vagrancy charges didn't stick, the court somehow connected Tuminaro and Lisi to the seven-month-old robbery.

By the 1950s, Tuminaro was well known to authorities as an organized crime member and was considered to be a "vicious killer" who was "constantly armed" and dangerous. He was running a "Greek Rummy" game out of an apartment on Second Avenue between Eleventh and Twelfth Streets, was part owner of the Apollo Barbershop at 144 Clinton Street and was dating a woman named Joan Motto, whose father, Danny Motto, was a reputed Lower East Side loan shark.

Angelo Tuminaro was a key figure in the Ormento-Galante-Mira-Di Pietro multimillion-dollar heroin-trafficking operation that sent most of the ring to prison in 1962. The original trial was set to begin on November 14, 1960; however, Tuminaro disappeared and failed to appear, moving the start of the trial to November 21. Tuminaro probably figured that if he could lie low for the duration of the trial, he would be acquitted on the most serious charges because it would be improbable that the same legal teams, witnesses, etc., would be assembled again for a single prosecution.[124]

The first trial ended in a mistrial, but a second (minus Tuminaro, still on the run) resulted in prosecutions for most of the codefendants. Right about the time of that trial, a separate police investigation was underway that would soon implicate Tuminaro in another international narcotics trafficking and distribution operation that would be immortalized in a bestselling book and hit 1970s Hollywood blockbuster of the same name.

In the original 1969 novel, *The French Connection: A True Account of Cops, Narcotics, and International Conspiracy*, author Robert Moore claimed that the investigation began on October 7, 1961, when NYPD detectives Eddie Egan, Sonny Grosso and Richard Auleita suspected a mobster named Pasquale "Patsy" Fuca of dealing heroin from his diner on Bushwick Avenue in Brooklyn. They were particularly suspicious of how Fuca could have afforded two cars and a housekeeper on a counterman's salary. When the FBI was consulted, the feds told the NYPD that Fuca was the nephew of reputed gangster and fugitive narcotics trafficker Angelo Tuminaro. The local police began an investigation into Fuca, hoping to be able to track down Tuminaro, but had no idea that they were about to uncover one of the most famous smuggling operations in history.

The NYPD started out by staking out Fuca's luncheonette and noticed several suspicious transactions taking place. Within weeks, over sixty local and federal law enforcement agents were performing twenty-four-hour, seven-day-a-week surveillance on Fuca and his ring, which included father Joseph, brother Tony (a longshoreman), mother Nellie (Tuminaro's sister) and teenage wife, Barbara (whose story was told in the 1977 book *Mafia Wife*, also by Robert Moore).

After a lengthy and sometimes disappointing investigation, authorities eventually traced Fuca back to an apartment in Brooklyn, where they uncovered twenty-five pounds of heroin, a submachine gun, two rifles, a shotgun and a bayonet in the basement, stashed behind freshly plastered walls. The rest is Mafia (and Hollywood) history.

Though the iconic 1974 movie captivated audiences and made the story a legend, in context, the French Connection sting yielded just a few lower-level convictions, did little to damage the Mafia's narcotics trafficking and distribution operations in the United States and failed to bring in alleged ringleader Angelo Tuminaro. In fact, the operation was said to continue after Fuca was arrested when Frank Tuminaro took over the operation for a short time, until he was indicted on trafficking charges, jumped bail and disappeared for a few years.

Angelo Tuminaro turned himself in to Federal Bureau of Narcotics agents in Miami, Florida, sometime in 1962 and made "an undisclosed deal" with authorities.[125] He would only spend four years behind bars before being released in 1966, and despite the notion that he had retired by the mid-1970s, Angelo Tuminaro was ranked forty-ninth on *Forbes*'s "Top 50 Mafia Bosses" in 1986.

On August 16, 1968, Little Angie's brother Frank turned up dead. He and associate Frank Joseph Gangi were found murdered in a rural area north of New York City; they had both been shot in the head, bound with rope and wrapped in plastic bags. An informant at the time told the FBI that Genovese soldier Charles "Chaultz" Gagliodotto, a former partner in the Tuminaro narcotics racket, was the triggerman and that the pair was lured to a Mott Street social club and murdered. Another informant backed up the story, adding that the pair was killed over a contested $17,000, and though the dispute was settled (in favor of Tuminaro and Gangi), Gagliodotto was furious and lured the two to their deaths. No one was ever charged in the murders, and Gagliodotto, perhaps in retaliation, was suffocated to death with a plastic bag on August 22.[126]

11
SOCIAL CLUBS AND HANGOUTS

ALBERTI BAKING COMPANY
441 East Twelfth Street, Corner of Avenue A

Mobster Andrew Alberti operated this business with his brother James in the 1940s and '50s. It was frequented by the East Village–based Genovese crew, led by Thomas Licatta and then Gus Frasca. The FBN believed Alberti inherited his father Frank's rackets when he passed away, though he had only one arrest on his record—a complaint for violation of narcotics laws in 1953—and that was dismissed. Today, the corner storefront hosts a coffee shop.

ALTO KNIGHTS SOCIAL CLUB
247 Mulberry Street

See Ravenite Social Club.

BARI RESTAURANT SUPPLY
240 Bowery Street, between Prince and East Houston Streets

On June 14, 1983, the FBI tracked mobster Sal Avellino's car from Long Island, New York, to this location, where a secret Mafia meeting was to take place. The feds' plan was to photograph attendees, but before they had a chance to establish surveillance positions, Paul Castellano (Gambino boss), Anthony Salerno (Genovese boss), Anthony "Ducks" Corallo (Lucchese boss) and other top-level Mafiosi fled from the building in different directions after Castellano noticed an FBI agent peering through the window. (This business still exists.)

BUS STOP LUNCHEONETTE

115 Madison Street, between Market and Catherine Streets

In the 1970s, this was a diner run by Bonanno soldier Anthony Mirra. It is the place where he first became friendly with Detective Joseph Pistone, aka Donnie Brasco. A Chinese restaurant has occupied this location for several years.

CAFFE DANTE

81 McDougal Street, between West Houston and Bleecker Streets

This is one of the few twentieth-century mob hangouts that still exists and retains much of the social club atmosphere once experienced by Genovese crime family members like Vincent "Chin" Gigante.

CAFFE PALERMO

148 Mulberry Street, between Hester and Grand Streets

This popular pasticceria, which still serves up some of the best cannolis around, was home base to suspected Gambino mobster Anthony DeLutro (who also allegedly ran an after-hours club called Sewer at 11 East Sixth Street), until he was sentenced to twenty years in prison in December 1975.

CAFFE ROMA

385 Broome Street, Corner of Mulberry Street

This pasticceria, a neighborhood staple since 1891, was part owned by mobsters Eli Zeccardi and Benedetto Cinquegrana in the 1950s. It was a regular haunt for Apalachin Conference attendee Carmine Lombardozzi.

CAMELOT SUPPER CLUB

158 East Forty-ninth Street

The Camelot, described by entertainer Clay Cole as a "tourist-trap with a hefty cover charge,"[127] was a popular and convenient spot for mobsters to rub elbows (and do business) with celebrities in the 1950s and '60s. In its heyday, the likes of the Ronnetts and the Capris performed for its well-connected audience, which included patrons like Liberace, Anne Margret and Merv Griffin. The club was operated by nightlife impresario "Joe the Wop" Cataldo and was the unofficial headquarters for the William Morris Agency's top booking agent, George Wood.

CARMELLO'S

1638 York Ave, between East Eighty-sixth and East Eighty-seventh Streets

This former dive bar and eatery was a popular hotspot for local wiseguys and was where "Donnie Brasco" got friendly with the mob by slowly injecting himself into backgammon games with the regulars under the guise of a jewel thief. The ground floor currently hosts a bagel store.

Celano's Garden

36 Kenmare Street, Corner of Elizabeth Street

This former unassuming restaurant on the corner of Kenmare and Elizabeth Streets was said to be the early 1930s headquarters for Charlie "Lucky" Luciano, who was accused of operating from this address the multimillion-dollar prostitution ring that earned him thirty to fifty years in prison and eventual deportation. The building has since been demolished.

CIA Club

72 Forsyth Street, between Hester and Grand Streets

In the 1950s and '60s, this former mob bar, which overlooks Sara D. Roosevelt Park, was partially owned by Gaetano Lisi and was popular with guys like Frank Mari and Carli Di Pietro. Today, the address hosts a pair of Chinese goods wholesalers.

Club 82

82 East Fourth Street, between Bowery Street and Second Avenue

Club 82, which is is featured in such films as *The Rose*, starring Bette Midler, and *Torch Song Trilogy*, with Harvey Fierstein, was one of New York City's most famous gay supper clubs, opened in 1953 by Genovese crime family associate Stephen Franse, a front for the mob in several mid-century New York City nightclubs. When Franse's Club 181 closed at 181 Second Avenue, he reopened at this location with the same management—which included boss Vito Genovese's own wife, Anna. Franse's job was to watch over Anna, who was divorcing Vito, but he may not have done a good enough job. On June 19, 1953, Franse was found dead in front of 164 East Thirty-seventh Street. Today, the building hosts a restaurant and sports bar.

COPACABANA

10 East Sixtieth Street, between Madison and Fifth Avenues

The legendary "Copa" was the hottest nightclub in New York City during the 1940s and '50s and hosted the biggest names in show business—Frank Sinatra, Dean Martin, Jerry Lewis, Sammy Davis Jr., Marvin Gaye and The Supremes, to name just a few. There was a time when an artist did not make it in show business unless he was successful at the Copa. A man named Monte Prosner was the owner and operator of the world-famous venue—on paper. However, it was widely known who was actually behind the club: mob kingpin Frank Costello. Prosner was also recruited for the same scheme at the Piping Rock in Saratoga, New York, an upscale supper club/resort just a few hours upstate from the city that shielded a massive gambling operation run by Meyer Lansky.

CUOMO CHEESE CORP

215 Mulberry Street, between Spring and Prince Streets

This former retailer of fine imported goods was a widely popular fixture in Little Italy for decades. It was also said to be a popular location for Peter DeFao to hold clandestine mob meetings in the 1980s. Presently, it is the site of a lingerie boutique.

DA NICO RESTAURANT

164 Mulberry Street, between Grand and Broome Streets

A local favorite to this day, Da Nico Ristorante was an alleged late 1990s headquarters of Bonnano crime family boss Richie "Shellackhead" Cantarella, the nephew of Alfred Embarrato and alleged murderer of Anthony Mirra.

De Robertis Pasticceria

176 First Avenue, between East Tenth and East Eleventh Streets

This century-old neighborhood treasure possesses a long and storied mob history. It was a favorite haunt of teenage Charlie Luciano, who lived around the corner on East Tenth Street, and the base of both Genovese and Gambino members for several decades.

By the 1950s, Gambino capo (and future underboss) Joseph "Piney" Armone allegedly based his operations out of the café. The FBI originally listed Armone as a Bonanno member, but I believe that has since been updated.

De Robertis was also a regular haunt of several Genovese crew members who grew up in the neighborhood: Anthony "Figgy" Ficcarota, Nicholas "Nicky the Blond" Frustaci and Enrico "Red Hot" Gentile. Ficcarota was once arrested for attempted murder of stool pigeon Vinny "the Cat" Siciliano, but he beat the rap. Frustaci was sponsored into the crew by good friend Victor Tramaglino. In 1997, he was convicted, along with Genovese consigliere Jimmy Ida, for conspiracy to murder and racketeering.

Gentile was behind the home invasion of a prominent New York family and pleaded guilty on July 20, 1966, to first-degree robbery, first-degree grand larceny, two counts of second-degree assault, felonious possession of a pistol and jumping bail. He was sentenced to fifteen to twenty years on the robbery indictment alone and sent to Attica State Prison (second floor, E Block), where he was shot in the leg during the infamous riot of 1971. Inside sources claim Gentile was the leader of the white inmate population at the time of the uprising.

After enduring a lifetime in gangland and surviving deadly, headline-making riots, Gentile succumbed to a heart attack in 2003 while getting on his motorcyle—in front of De Robertis Café.

By the early 1990s, De Robertis was placed under FBI surveillance to track the goings-on of John "Handsome Jack" Giordano, a Gambino capo who was allegedly responsible for some of John Gotti's biggest rackets. Giordano inherited his uncle Joseph Armone's East Village crew in the 1980s and continued its operations from a small office in the back of the café.

The feds picked up phone conversations pertaining to everything from bookmaking, loan-sharking and gambling to illicit activities at the

San Gennaro Festival. That was peanuts compared to the $300 million sports-betting ring, of which Giordano was the center. Superbowls, NBA playoffs—you name it. It was a high-end, sophisticated operation that earned Giordano several criminal indictments in 1991.

Giordano tried convincing the court that he was employed as a wrangler at a dude ranch. Judge Raymond Harrington stated, "If you thought I'd believe that, you must think I'm another part of a horse's anatomy,"[128] before sentencing him to four to twelve years behind bars.

De Robertis Café, once one of the neighborhood's best-kept secrets, is today a family-run (mob-free) tourist destination. However, most people visit for some of the best pastries in the city—and have no idea of its secret history.

Fretta's Meat Market

116 Mott Street, Corner of Hester Street

According to undercover detective Joseph Pistone, aka Donnie Brasco, a Bananno crew held high-stakes card games above this former neighborhood staple, which closed in the 1990s. The address has since been occupied by Chinese retail merchants.

Gatsby's

20 East Forty-first Street, between Madison and Fifth Avenues

A favorite high-end restaurant of Frank Costello, this was where the "retired" mob kingpin was seen holding meetings with Charles Tourine in 1970, possibly advising the family he once ruled after the death of its boss, Vito Genovese. Today, the address hosts a Japanese restaurant known for its authentic shaved-ice cocktails.

Gold Key Club
28 West Fifty-sixth Street

Owned by Anthony Strollo (according to Joe Valachi) and operated by Vincent Mauro (according to authorities), the Gold Key Club, opened in 1950, was New York City's premier, high-society, after-hours bottle club—until the city had it shut down in 1956.

The über-swanky (and über-expensive) hot spot attracted only the most prominent clientele. According to the FBI files on Frank Sinatra, the Gold Key Club was the place the superstar entertainer frequented when in New York City. In fact, Mauro and Anthony Strollo threw an elaborate going-away party here for the singer in the winter of 1955, just before he embarked on a tour of Australia.

There were four types of memberships offered by the semiexclusive speakeasy, from free for celebrities, mobsters and important businessmen to "Super-Special Sucker" memberships, which cost said suckers sixty dollars per year just to enter the place. At its height, the club boasted thirty-five hundred members.

The club endured a handful of raids in the early 1950s and an October 1952 face slashing of actor/singer Billy Daniels, at the hands of Vincent Mauro. Despite the negative publicity, business thrived until a final raid on February 10, 1956.

At 4:45 a.m., police entered the Gold Key Club and apprehended seventeen staff members for questioning, including Vincent Mauro. Anthony Strollo was picked up a few blocks away in his car, and sixty patrons were handed subpoenas to appear in court.

On May 21, 1957, the club, and Vincent Mauro, pleaded guilty to storing liquor with the intent to sell without a license, and the short-lived but legendary venue was closed for good.

Hawaiian Moonlighters Social Club

141 Mulberry, between Hester and Grand Streets

Formally known as the Andrea Doria Social Club, this was a longtime Gambino crime family headquarters run by Joseph "Butch" Corrao. In 1993, two low-level ex-cons named Thomas and Rosemarie Uva decided to rob the patrons of this address armed with a machine gun. Despite being warned by customers, the couple got away with this act, not once, but twice, before Mafia justice ended the wannabe Bonnie and Clyde's adventure. On Christmas Eve 1993, the pair was found murdered in their car on 103rd Avenue and 91st Street. Today, a touristy Italian-style restaurant occupies the address.

141 Mulberry Street today.
Courtesy of Shirley Dluginski.

HIPPOPOTAMUS

405 East Sixty-second Street, between First and York Avenues

This once world-famous 1970s and '80s dance club was a regular haunt for partying mobsters to rub elbows with a mixed clientele of hip celebrities (like Mick Jagger) and up-and-coming "club kids" (like Steve Ruben of Studio 54 fame). The Hippopotamus opened at its original location (154 East Fifty-fourth Street) about 1970 and was owned by French nightlife pioneer Olivier Coquelin, who was already famous for New York City hot spots Le Club, Ondine and the Cheetah. A May 1970 *New York Magazine* advertises the Hippopotamus as "a new pleasure palace with Poonah bar, Mantra garden, dancing, dining, drinking, divans, psychedelia."

Joe Pistone was officially introduced to a Colombo crime family member here, in January 1977, and gangster turned informer Henry Hill said in his book, *A Goodfella's Guide to New York*, "If I stepped in there in its early '80s reign I would have been killed in ten minutes tops."

Currently, this is the site of an eleven-story apartment complex.

HOLIDAY BAR

116 Madison Street, between Market and Catherine Streets

This was a regular haunt for Benjamin "Lefty Guns" Ruggiero and Anthony Mirra, who owned the Bus Stop Luncheonette across the street. Joe Pistone described it as "the only place he [Ruggiero] could really let his hair down" and as "a place so dingy, [he] would only drink beer or club soda out of a bottle" during his undercover investigation in the 1970s. A Chinese wholesaler has occupied the space for several years.

116 Madison Street today. *Courtesy of Sachiko Akama.*

Holiday Inn Bar & Restaurant

55 Madison Street, Corner of Olive Street

This mid-century mob hangout (no relation to the Holiday Bar at 116 Madison, which came later) was a popular meeting place for Bonnano mobsters and was co-owned by Gaetano Lisi. Currently, it is the site of a pharmacy.

House of Chan

800 Seventh Avenue, between West Fifty-second and West Fifty-third Streets

This was a 1950s and '60s haunt for celebrities, the after-theater crowd, tourists and gangsters like Carlo Gambino, Angelo Bruno and Joe Colombo. Today, the address hosts a supper club and event rental space.

Jay's Bar

49 East Houston Street, between Mott and Mulberry Streets

This was yet another 1950s dive bar under Gaetano Lisi's control, frequented by members of the Bonanno organization. This building was recently demolished.

Jilly's

256 West Fifty-second Street, between Broadway and Eighth Avenue

Jilly's was said to have been popular with gangsters, entertainers and politicians (like Vice President Spiro Agnew). Today, it is the site of an upscale Russian restaurant and vodka bar.

JOHN'S RESTAURANT
302 East Eleventh Street, between First and Second Avenues

This century-old neighborhood favorite was a hot spot for local mobsters early in the twentieth century and the site of Umberto Rocco Valenti's murder in 1922, allegedly at the hands of a young Charlie Luciano (though no one was ever convicted of the crime). It was in retaliation for the failed hit on Giuseppe Masseria just days earlier at 82 Second Avenue.

Carlo Tresca, a good friend of the original owner, lived above the restaurant, and it was the last place he dined on the evening of his murder. (See Tresca, Carlo, "Ganglant Hits" chapter.)

John's later became a favorite eatery for celebrities like John Lennon. Madonna worked there as a waitress before becoming a star, and it has played backdrop to several movies and television shows, including *The Sopranos*.

Today, crowds flock to John's for century-old atmosphere and some of the most authentic Italian cooking left in the city. What are you waiting for? Tell Nick I sent you.

JOY'S RESTAURANT
28 Spring Street, Corner of Mott Street

This former restaurant on the corner of Mott Street was a favorite 1950s hangout of one-third of the fearsome Beck Brothers—Charlie DiPalermo. It is now the site of a retail market.

KNOTTY PINE SOCIAL CLUB
221 Mulberry Street (Lower East Side)

This was a popular members-only club through at least the 1980s, frequented by Peter DeFeo and Genovese boss Alphonse Frank "Funzi" Tieri.

La Donna Rosa Restaurant

19 Cleveland Place, between Kenmare and Spring Streets

This restaurant was owned and operated by former Lucchese crime family acting boss Alphonso "Little Al" D'Arco before he turned on the mob in 1991 and became a witness in several high-profile trials that sent many of his old friends to prison, including Vincent "Chin" Gigante. The storefront space, ironically overlooking Lieutenant Petrosino Square, today hosts a Mexican restaurant.

Lombardi's Restaurant

53 Spring Street, between Mulberry and Lafayette Streets

This former local eatery was a favorite hangout for men like Thomas Eboli and Peter DeFeo. It is now home to a 1920s retro-style sports bar and lounge.

Longchamp's Restaurant

19 West Fifty-seventh Street, between Fifth and Sixth Avenues

In April 1942, mob kingpin Meyer Lansky met two men at Longchamp's for a breakfast meeting: New York assistant district attorney Murray Gurfein and Moses Polakoff, a lawyer who represented Charlie Luciano in his 1936 trial. According to legend, the pair requested the mobster's help in urging Luciano, who was serving time in prison, to assist U.S. Naval Intelligence in the war effort. This is now the site of a multi-lot, mixed-use, glass skyscraper.

Luna's Restaurant

112 Mulberry Street, between Canal and Hester Streets

This one-time neighborhood favorite was frequented by mobsters like "Crazy" Joey Gallo, who, according to controversial New York columnist and author Jimmy Breslin, walked in one evening with a live lion on a chain.[129] Operating in the space today is a gift shop geared toward tourists.

LUXOR BATHS

121 West Forty-sixth Street, between Sixth and Seventh Avenues

This was a favorite spa for later twentieth-century Mafioso to hold business meetings—in the steam room, where bugs could not be transmitted. Today, a high-rise office building occupies the address.

MANFREDI'S RESTAURANT

331 East 108th Street, between 1st and 2nd Avenues

Manfredi's was owned by Joseph Manfredi, a key East Harlem–based mobster who served seven years in the 1960s for narcotics laws violations. The address, close to First Avenue and the East River at the edge of a gentrifying Hispanic neighborhood, hosts an apartment building today.

MILADY'S BAR

167 Bleecker Street, Corner of Sullivan Street

This 1950s mob hangout was frequented by Innocenzio "Johnny the Bug" Stoppelli, as well as Jewish mobster and convicted heroin smuggler Nathan Behrman (Berman). It is now the site of a nightclub.

The southwest corner of Elizabeth and Prince Streets today. *Courtesy of Shirley Dluginski.*

MUSICAL CLUB

18 Prince Street, Corner of Elizabeth Street

This former social club, located on the corner of Elizabeth Street, was another Genovese hangout frequented by Bonanno family boss Carmine Galante in the mid-twentieth century. A retail store recently moved into the space.

NAPOLI E NOTTE CAFÉ

165 Thompson Street, between Bleecker and West Third Streets

This is where high-ranking Mafiosi like Jerry Catena, Thomas Eboli and Michael Miranda sipped espresso and made no bones about it. A sign on the door once said, "This is not a club. Don't hang around." As of this writing, the storefront is under renovation.

PALMA BOYS SOCIAL CLUB

416 East 115th Street, between 1st and Pleasant Avenues

This was the East Harlem headquarters of Genovese crime family boss Anthony Salerno. By 1985, the FBI had gathered enough information from a bug on the premises—like business conversations between Salerno, Mattie Ianniello and Anthony Corallo—to help indict several members of the Mafia in what became known as the Mafia Commission trial. Today, the four-story building hosts a small retail space.

PANEL SOCIAL CLUB

208 Thompson Street, between Bleecker and West Third Streets

This was another Genovese hangout during the reign of Vincent "Chin" Gigante. An unassuming yet popular Italian restaurant has occupied the address for the last few decades.

PARNELL SOCIAL CLUB

224 East 112th Street, between 2nd and 3rd Avenues

Now the site of an apartment complex, this address once hosted a popular club frequented by several East Harlem mobsters in the 1950s, including one Mafioso with the peculiar name Theodore Roosevelt Orzo.

PATRISSY'S RESTAURANT

98 Kenmare Street, between Center and Mulberry Streets

This former neighborhood staple, opened in 1906, was a favorite of Charlie Luciano. The gangster was said to have regularly dined with the likes of Second Assembly District leader (and New York county clerk) Al Marinelli, whose offices were close by at 225 Lafayette Street (curiously, in the same building as "Jimmy Doyle" Plumeri's Five Borough Truckmen's Association). Marinelli was a powerful Tammany politician who shielded much of the mob's operations in the 1930s, before being brought down by Thomas E. Dewey in 1938. The corrupt politico became close with Johnny Torrio as a young man in the 1910s during their days running various illegal rackets in Little Italy and was said to have been propped up by Torrio and "Socks" Lanza in his 1931 State Assembly election. Today, you can order "fresh homemade" kebabs and falafel from the restaurant on the premises.

Ravenite Social Club

247 Mulberry Street, between Prince and Spring Streets

Perhaps the most famous Mafia social club in America, 247 Mulberry will forever be associated with the "Dapper Don," John Gotti Sr.—the Gambino

247 Mulberry Street today.
Courtesy of Shirley Dluginski.

boss who spent much of his time at this address through the early 1990s. However, the criminal history of this building goes back many decades.

Originally known as the Alto Knights Social Club dating back to 1926, when it is said Charlie "Lucky" Luciano was a patron. The title was changed in the 1950s by Carlo Gambino, who renamed it the Raven Knights Social Club—supposedly after his favorite poem, "The Raven" by Edgar Allen Poe. By the time Gambino's underboss, Aniello Dellacroce, was running the crew in the 1970s, the name had morphed into "Ravenite." When Dellacroce passed away in 1985, Gotti Sr. would inherit this Mafia landmark by assuming control of the Gambinos after Paul Castellano was murdered.

By 1992, federal authorities had gathered enough evidence on Gotti to indict him on several charges. Surveillance on the Ravenite, where he was recorded discussing family business, contributed to the case against Gotti.

In October 1997, the FBI finally seized control of the building, ending a seventy-year run of remarkable Mafia history. Today, the storefront hosts a retail store.

Reno Bar

168 Elizabeth Street, between Spring and Kenmare Streets

What has been a Chinese laundry for several years was at one time a mid-century dive bar and regular haunt for Mafiosi like the Beck (Di Palermo) Brothers.

Shoreview Social Club

413–15 East Twelfth Street, between First Avenue and Avenue A

This was the longtime headquarters for mob boss Joseph Bonanno. The unassuming ground floor-locale was fortified with a steel door, and its storefront windows were lined with plasterboard to prevent curious eyes from peeking inside. Outside on the curb was a fire hydrant that served no other purpose than to ensure parking for VIPs (let's just say that it wasn't placed there by the city).

According to Bill Bonanno, Joseph's son, "Someone told me once that the quality of a social club could be measured by the availability of food and quality of the complaints. By that standard the Shoreview was a good place to belong."[130] The storefront has been completely renovated and hosts one of the few remaining vinyl record stores in the city.

SKYLINE MOTOR INN

725 Tenth Avenue, between West Forty-ninth and West Fiftieth Streets

This decades-old economy motel was said to be the 1960s/'70s Manhattan headquarters for Brooklyn-based Gambino soldier Roy Albert DeMeo.

SPRING VALLEY PLEASURE CLUB

238 Elizabeth Street, between Prince and East Houston Streets

This very secret, second-floor, members-only club was frequented by Carmine Galante in the early twentieth century. The Albanese Meat Market on the ground floor has been in operation since 1924 and is one of the last traditional mom-and-pop businesses in the neighborhood. Director Martin Scorsese, who grew up across the street at 253 Elizabeth (next door to my father), filmed a scene here for his first full-length feature film in 1967, titled *Who's That Knocking at My Door*.

SQUEEZE INN

57 East Fourth Street, between Bowery Street and Second Avenue

This bar, owned by Ralph Polizzano, was one of several key distribution points for the international heroin-trafficking ring that sent Polizzano, Carmine Galante and several others to prison in 1961. The building is now entirely residential.

238 Elizabeth Street today. *Courtesy of Sachiko Akama.*

57 East Fourth Street today. *Courtesy of Sachiko Akama.*

STAGE BAR

89 East Fourth Street, between Bowery Street and Second Avenue

This mid-century mob hangout was owned by Vincent Ciraulo, who was known as "Jimmy Second Avenue," and attracted much of the same crowd as the Squeeze Inn a few doors away. Today, the address hosts a popular and affordable Italian restaurant.

SUGAR BOWL

305 Broome Street, between Forsyth and Eldridge Streets

The sandwich shop that currently occupies the ground floor once hosted one of the many bars in which Frank Mari was said to hold interest by the 1960s.

THOMPSON STREET SOCIAL CLUB

21 Prince Street, between Elizabeth and Mott Streets

This address hosted an important Genovese crime family members-only club for several decades in the late twentieth century. Today, a designer clothing store occupies the premises. According to one web reviewer, the store "had the one-day sale of all the leftover wardrobe from *Sex and the City* (I'm a HUGE *Sex and the City* fan!)" Welcome to twenty-first-century Little Italy—excuse me, "NoLita."

TONY PASTOR'S CLUB

130 West Third Street, between Sixth Avenue and MacDougal Street

This was another very popular mid-century nightspot operated by Joseph Cataldo and frequented by several Mafiosi. Tony Pastor is the name of the show business pioneer who helped popularize vaudeville in the 1880s. There

21 Prince Street today.
Courtesy of Sachiko Akama.

is no word on whether this club's name is a tribute to him. The space has hosted another popular live music venue named the Village Underground for about the last decade.

TRIANGLE SOCIAL CLUB

208 Sullivan Street, between Bleecker and West Third Streets

Officially named the Triangle Civic Improvement Association, this was the longtime headquarters of Vincent "Chin" Gigante, the Genovese boss who feigned mental illness for over three decades. Today, the building is occupied by a tea and spice retailer.

VIVERE LOUNGE

199 Second Avenue, between East Twelfth and East Thirteenth Streets

Operated by Carli Di Pietro, the Vivere was at the center of the Galante-Ormento-Mirra narcotics operation. It was where Montreal Mafia representatives were allegedly introduced to Anthony Mirra while being wooed by the New York mob during the spring of 1958. Mirra, at that time, was working under John Ormento and was suspected of overseeing the ring's Midtown East operations. On June 24, Canadian crime boss Giuseppe "Pepe" Cotroni himself made a trip to New York and visited the Vivere to meet with Di Pietro, according to court records.

The Vivere was said to be the first stop in one of five heroin-distribution routes that serviced the Greater New York area. On this route, couriers would allegedly deliver street-ready heroin in small travel bags or suitcases on an almost weekly basis to Di Pietro at this location, before stopping next at the Squeeze Inn on East Fourth Street and then heading into Brooklyn. A hair salon has occupied the premises for several years.

III
GANGLAND HITS

ALFANO, PIETRO

East Side of Sixth Avenue between Eighth and Ninth Streets

On February 11, 1987, two men stepped out of a red Chevy near the corner of Sixth Avenue and West Ninth Street, where fifty-seven-year-old pizza shop owner Pietro Alfano was exiting the old Balducci's market (424 Sixth Avenue) with his wife and bags of groceries in tow. The pair followed Alfano south for a few yards before one of them pulled out a .38-caliber revolver and fired three shots into his back. When Alfano dropped to the ground, the gunman opened fire on an innocent bystander before fleeing north on foot, back toward West Ninth Street. One assassin jumped in a yellow cab and the other in a blue van, disappearing into the busy downtown traffic.

When thirty-three-year-old Philip Ragosta and forty-one-year-old Frank Bavosa were arrested the the next day, they admitted to receiving $10,000 each for the hit, plus at least $10,000 in expenses, according to the FBI. It turned out that the pair had been following Alfano for months, waiting for the right opportunity to murder him.

A mob connection was quickly established by authorities. Alfano was no ordinary businessman. He was the nephew of Gaetano Badalamenti, a notorious Sicilian Mafia leader at the center of what was called the Pizza Connection case. The shooting victim was a defendant on trial in the infamous case, suspected of being the American point man for a $1.6 billion international heroin-trafficking ring that used pizza shops across the United States as distribution points.

This was the second such shooting related to the case. On December 3 of that year, the body of Gaetano Mazzara, another defendant in the trial, was found in a garbage bag in Brooklyn. However, both Alfano and bystander Ronald Price miraculously survived the nearly point-blank-range hit attempt; organized crime strike force prosecutor Robert Stewart chalked this up to "bad shooting."[131]

The attempt on his life may have been a bizarre blessing in disguise for Alfano, who faced life in prison without parole in the Pizza Connection trial. His case was declared a mistrial in July 1987 because he missed the last eighteen days of the seventeen-month trial due to his injuries. None of his eighteen U.S. codefendants fared so well, and all were sentenced to lengthy terms in March 1987.

Those connected to the Sicilian side of the case were not so lucky. Attorney for the U.S. Senate Permanent Investigations Subcommittee Harriet McFaul claimed that "twenty-two police chiefs, judges, politicians and Mafia hunters were murdered before the trial on the so-called Italian end of the Pizza Connection case."[132]

ANASTASIA, ALBERT

870 Seventh Avenue, Park Sheraton Hotel

At about 10:20 a.m. on the morning of October 25, 1957, Anastasia was relaxing in a barber chair at this address (now the Park Central Hotel) when two men slipped in the front door, quietly pushed the barber aside and fired several shots at the veteran mobster. Their target, disoriented, stood up and returned fire at his own reflection in the mirror before collapsing on the floor and dying of his wounds. One of the gunmen dropped his .38-caliber Colt revolver, with five spent shots, in the hotel lobby while fleeing. Another revolver was found four hours later in the subway station beneath the hotel; this weapon had only been fired once. Despite the efforts of over one hundred law enforcement officials originally assigned to the case, this assassination remains officially unsolved. However, gangland chatter pointed to "Crazy" Joey Gallo and his brother.

Anastasia had fallen out of favor with the mob and was marked for death by the early 1950s, but the powers that be offered the powerful gangster a chance to live if he retired and relocated from the city. Spending most of the 1950s underground in his Fort Lee, New Jersey home, Anastasia began pushing his luck by frequenting New York City more and more in the months before his death.

Coincidentally, this is the same address where gambler and racketeer Arnold Rothstein was shot on November 4, 1928, in room 349, dying hours later. That murder is also unsolved.

BARETTO, GREGARIO
636 East Thirteenth Street

On July 6, 1971, twenty-nine-year-old Gregario Baretto was shot in the chest by an unknown gunman on the sidewalk at this location near Avenue D. Authorities believed the shooting was part of a brewing war for control of the Colombo family, though Baretto, in critical condition, refused to identify his attacker or cooperate with a police investigation.

BILOTTI, THOMAS
210 East Forty-sixth Street, Sparks Steak House

As bodyguard to Paul Castellano, Thomas Bilotti (March 23, 1940– December 16, 1985) became an unfortunate casualty in John Gotti's drive to become boss of the Gambino crime family. (See Castellano, Paul, below.)

BONANNO, JOSEPH
Park Avenue at East Thirty-fifth Street

At close to midnight on October 20, 1964, mob boss Joe Bonanno (January 18, 1905–May 11, 2002) was getting out of a car in front of his lawyer's apartment building at this location when two men forced him into the backseat of a waiting vehicle. Bonanno was held captive in an upstate farmhouse for six weeks before being driven to Texas and released unharmed. The veteran mobster then spent over a year hiding out in the Southwest, disguised in a beard.

At least, that is the story according to Joe Bonanno. Most law enforcement officials and Mafia insiders seriously doubt the kidnapping ever took place. Conveniently for Bonanno, due to the "abduction," he missed having to testify before a grand jury on October 21 or face incarceration for contempt of court.

Prison time was the least of Bonanno's troubles. He made a lot of enemies when an alleged plot to murder fellow family bosses Carlo Gambino and Gaetano Lucchese was uncovered. Many theorize that Bonanno fled the city in order to figure out a way to make peace with the Mafia Commission, which was furious over Bonanno's unsanctioned plan.

Joe Bonanno inherited the family in 1931 and ran it for three decades in relative peace until the early 1960s. His troubles are said to have begun when a popular longtime capo named Gaspar DiGregorio was passed over for a consigliere position in favor of Bonanno's own son, Salvatore "Bill" Bonanno, causing a rift in the family.

When Joe Bonanno disappeared in 1964, the commission stepped in and appointed DiGregorio acting boss by 1965, infuriating supposed successor Bill Bonanno and his supporters. The resulting "Bonanno War" turned violent as loyalists to both men chose sides and fought for control of the family.

Most of the hostilities ended by 1968, when Joe Bonanno suffered a heart attack and officially retired his throne. Battling factions had united by the end of the decade under the leadership of Natale Evola, who also helped mend the family's relationship with the Gambinos and Luccheses.

Briguglio, Salvatore

163 Mulberry Street

At about 11:15 p.m. on June 26, 1978, two unidentified men approached forty-eight-year-old Genovese crime family soldier "Sally Bugs" Briguglio on the sidewalk outside the Benito's II restaurant at this address and knocked him to the ground before firing five bullets into his head and one into his chest.

Briguglio was a business agent for the International Brotherhood of Teamsters, Local 560, based out of Union City, New Jersey. At the time of his murder, prosecutors were building a case against Briguglio and Genovese capo Anthony "Tony Pro" Provenzano, implicating the mobsters in the 1961 slaying of rival teamster Anthony Castellito (whose body was never found and was said to have been put through a wood chipper).

The relationship between labor unions and the mob date back to the early twentieth century and perhaps peaked by the late 1950s, when the McClellan Committee began its investigations into organized crime. By 1960, newly appointed attorney general Robert Kennedy had targeted the International Brotherhood of Teamsters, Chauffeurs, Warehousemen and Helpers of America and its president, James Riddle Hoffa. When the organization's books were opened, investigators found several known Mafia members on the payroll, including Briguglio.

CASTELLANO, PAUL

210 East Forty-sixth Street

At about 5:30 p.m. on December 16, 1985, seventy-year-old Gambino boss Paul Castellano pulled up to the Sparks Steak House in a black Lincoln limo driven by bodyguard Thomas Bilotti. When the pair began to exit the

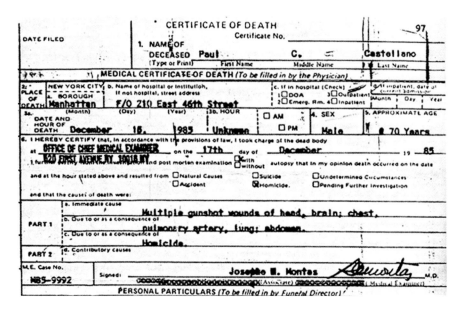

A portion of Paul Castellano's death certificate.

vehicle, three men walked up to them and opened fire with semiautomatic pistols. Each target took six shots to the head and body and collapsed on the street in pools of blood. Two gunmen sprinted down Forty-sixth Street, while one stayed behind briefly to ensure that the job was done, firing a single shot at point blank range into Castellano's skull before fleeing.

According to infamous Mafia turncoat Salvatore "the Bull" Gravano, he and John Gotti sat in a car nearby and observed the whole incident, which took no longer than thirty seconds to execute. Gravano recounted, "I believe Paul was shot first. Tommy squatted down to look through the window, kind of squatted down. And then somebody came up behind him and shot him. He [Bilotti] was actually watching Paul get shot."[133]

Gotti became boss of the Gambino family after the murder of Castellano, a position he would hold, even from behind bars, until his death in prison on June 10, 2002, at age sixty-one.

COLL, VINCENT

314 West Twenty-third Street

At about 12:45 a.m. on February 8, 1932, Vincent "Mad Dog" Coll and a bodyguard entered the London Chemists pharmacy at this address and headed to a phone booth in the rear of the store. Moments later, a man casually walked in through the front door and approached the booth Coll was standing in. Coll's bodyguard quietly took off at the sight of a Thompson submachine gun slung under the would-be killer's right arm, leaving his twenty-four-year-old boss to fend for himself.

According to witnesses, the gunman caught Coll off guard when he approached the phone booth and said, "Turn around Vincent, and get ready for it. I'm going to give it to you."[134] Coll had no chance. He was slaughtered by a hail of bullets from the powerful automatic weapon at close range. One slug tore away his entire nose, and several passed through his body completely.

The sensational murder took place across the street from the Cornish Arms Apartment building at 311–23 West Twenty-third Street, where Coll had been holed up and eventually arrested months earlier for killing a child during a hit attempt on rival Joey Rao on July 28, 1931.

Police guard the London Pharmacy where Vincent "Mad Dog" Coll was gunned down, 1932. *Library of Congress.*

Coll's slaying was said to have been ordered by bootlegging kingpin Owney Madden and carried out by hired guns Leonard Scarnici, Anthony Fabrizzo and Abraham "Bo" Weinberg. Scarnici later admitted to the crime before he was electrocuted at Sing Sing prison for the 1933 murder of a police detective.

Just five months before his murder, Vincent Coll (July 20, 1908–February 8, 1932) was approached by Mafia boss-of-all-bosses Salvatore Maranzano to kill Charlie Luciano. That plan did not quite work out (see Maranzano, Salvatore, below).

COLOMBO, JOSEPH, SR.

Columbus Circle, West Fifty-ninth Street at Central Park West

On Monday, June 28, 1971, mob boss Joe Colombo (December 14, 1914–May 22, 1978) was set to give a speech to the thousands who gathered at

Columbus Circle for an outdoor Italian Unity Day rally. As Colombo was shaking hands on his way to the stage, an African American man approached the veteran mobster and said "Hello Joe," before grabbing him by the neck and firing three bullets into his head at point-blank range.

The shooter, Jerome A. Johnson of New Brunswick, New Jersey—disguised as a reporter, with press pass and camera—was shot and killed at the scene by an unidentified gunman. Colombo was rushed to nearby Roosevelt Hospital, where doctors worked for six hours to save his life. They were successful; however, Colombo remained in a semi-comatose state until his death in 1978.

Several theories surround the motive of the shooting, which remains unsolved officially. Gangland legend has it that "Crazy Joey" Gallo was behind the murder, in hopes of taking over the family. An alternate leading theory is that fellow Mafiosi like Carlo Gambino were behind the assassination attempt. Yet another theory implicates the U.S. government.

D'AQUILA, SALVATORE

211 Avenue A, at East Thirteenth Street

In the early evening of October 10, 1928, "just as the [street] lamps were being lit,"[135] Prohibition-era Mafia boss Salvatore "Toto" D'Aquila met his maker in a hail of bullets while standing beside his car on the corner outside this address.

The murder put to rest a long-standing feud with Giuseppe "the Boss" Masseria, which dated back to at least 1922. D'Aquila was the top guy in the Italian underworld until Masseria began moving in on the gangster's bootlegging territory with the help of men like Giuseppe Morello, Charlie Luciano and Vito Genovese.

When D'Aquila was killed, Masseria declared himself "boss of bosses," a title he would hold for about three years before being murdered himself.

DiBono, Louis

Former Site of the World Trade Center

At 3:00 p.m. on October 4, 1990, a parking attendant of an underground garage at the World Trade Center discovered the body of sixty-three-year-old Louis DiBono lying across the front seat of his 1987 Cadillac. The three-hundred-plus-pound construction contractor and Gambino crime family member had been shot three times in the head.

Ten months before the murder, authorities recorded a phone call between Gambino boss John Gotti Sr. and an associate. In the conversation, Gotti said of DiBono, "He's gonna die because he refused to come in when I called...He didn't do nothing else wrong."[136]

Mafia turncoat Salvatore "the Bull" Gravano later testified that Gotti had targeted his underling because he felt disrespected.

Twenty-nine years later, in March 2009, mob hit man Charles Carneglia was found guilty of murdering four men over three decades, including Louis DiBono in 1990. Carneglia, a Gambino soldier, was sentenced to life in prison.

Gallina, Gino

Carmine Street, near Varick Street

Bronx-born Gino Gallina was a former New York assistant district attorney turned high-profile lawyer who had defended some of the most influential gangsters of the 1960s; however, his intimate relationship with the mob may have cost him his life.

Gallina served in the district attorney's office from 1965 through 1969 before taking on such infamous clients as Genovese crime family members and "American Gangster" Frank Lucas. According to at least one informer, Gallina was a successful defender because he passed on sealed information to his clients, which led to the murders of several witnesses (though these accusations were never proven).[137]

Gallina was accused in 1975 of being involved in an international heroin-trafficking ring and named as a co-conspirator in a federal trial alongside several organized crime figures; however, he was not indicted.

Whatever his relationship with the mob was, it deteriorated by 1977. On November 5 of that year, Gallina and a young female companion left a West Twenty-third Street restaurant shortly after 10:00 p.m. and headed to a downtown nightclub. As the couple was getting out of their car, parked on Carmine Street, an unidentified gunman stepped out of the shadows and shot Gallina seven times in the head and neck, in what was thought to be a mob hit. He died ninety minutes later at St. Vincent's Hospital on Sixth Avenue. The young woman was struck with a ricocheting bullet but survived.

Shortly before his death, Gallina had testified before a Newark grand jury that he held in his possession a secret tape recording that could prove who killed Jimmy Hoffa; however, he never had the chance to produce it.

GALLO, JOEY

129 Mulberry Street

On April 7, 1972, Colombo dissenter "Crazy Joey" Gallo was celebrating his forty-third birthday with some friends at the old Umberto's Clam House at this address when a gunman calmly walked up to the group and fired two shots into Gallo's head as he sat at his table. Gallo attempted to chase his assailant out the front door but stumbled several times before collapsing in the street and dying. At least one "bystander" returned fire on the assassin, who was able to escape unharmed.

The Gallo party had just returned to Little Italy for a late-night meal after a night on the town, which included a Don Rickels performance at the Copacabana. Seated at the table when Gallo was shot was his new wife, Sina; her ten-year-old daughter; and several relatives and close friends.

Joe Gallo (April 7, 1929–April 7, 1972), perhaps most famously known as the suspected killer of mob kingpin Albert Anastasia, was a member of the Joe Profaci crime family. By 1960, he had earned quite a high profile among police and Mafiosi alike for his truly brazen tactics. For example, when Gallo felt that Profaci—his boss and one of the most powerful Mafiosi in America—was shortchanging his crew, Gallo simply kidnapped Profaci's top four men (and attempted, but failed, to kidnap the boss himself).

The Gallo brothers—Larry, Albert and Joe—along with a dedicated crew of followers, had initiated what would become known as the Gallo-

129 Mulberry Street today. *Courtesy of Shirley Dluginski.*

Profaci War. After a few years of upheaval within the family, the war died down when Gallo was sent to prison in 1964 on charges of extortion. When released in 1971, Joey Gallo demanded what he felt was owed from the Profaci organization—only by this time, Joe Profaci had died and the new boss was Joe Colombo, who had no intention of paying Gallo reparations.

While in prison, Gallo formed relationships with black gang members and is said to have been one of the first to realize the value of incorporating urban street gangs into the Mafia's illegal activities. It was in fact an African American gunman who shot Joe Colombo three times in the head on June 28, 1971, in Columbus Circle. The gunman was suspected to have been working for Gallo, but no proof of a connection has ever been shown.

GIANNINI, EUGENIO

221 East 107th Street

In the early morning of September 20, 1952, the body of Gagliano/ Lucchese crime family member Eugenio "Gene" Giannini was found in

East 107th Street today. *Courtesy of Shirley Dluginski.*

the gutter in front of this address with two gunshot wounds to his head. It was determined that Giannini was shot about five blocks away in front of the Jefferson Majors Athletic Club at 2173 Second Avenue. From there, two associates tried driving the severely wounded mobster to the hospital, but when they realized he had died en route, they simply dumped his body out of the car at this location and fled. His sixteen-year-old son identified the body.

Upon investigation, it turned up that Giannini, a Calbrian immigrant, had been working as an informant for the FBI. According to the 1969 testimony of Joe Valachi, the orders to kill the forty-two-year-old turncoat—who shot and killed a police officer in 1934—came from the very top, meaning the exiled Charlie Luciano, who told Vito Genovese that the doomed mobster had been "talking to the junk agents [the Federal Bureau of Narcotics] for years," and "he had to be hit." Valachi was given the contract to kill Giannini, who in turned recruited his sister's son, twenty-five-year-old Fiore Siano, and two other up-and-coming gangsters, Joseph and Pasquale "Pat" Pagano.

According to Valachi, he drove the getaway car, and Siano did the shooting.

GIORDANO, JOHN

100 East Seventy-seventh Street

On the evening of April 11, 1995, fifty-five-year-old Gambino capo "Handsome Jack" Giordano paid a visit to ailing fellow mobster Louis DiFazio, a patient of the Lenox Hill Hospital at this location.

At 7:19 p.m., Giordano left the hospital and and set out toward a dark blue 1994 Chrysler sedan, parked in front of the hospital on Seventy-seventh Street near Park Avenue. As he was climbing into the passenger side of the vehicle, a slow-moving car crept by and fired a barrage of bullets at the mob leader, hitting him three times. One of the bullets severed Giordano's spine. He survived but was paralyzed from the waist down.

Giordano—who ran his crew out of De Robertis Pasticceria—was a close and trusted associate of John Gotti Sr. During the "Teflon Don's" 1990 federal racketeering trial, Giordano visited his boss regularly for moral support, and the pair often had coffee together during breaks.

Investigators later theorized that the shooting grew out of a dispute over a loan-sharking debt, and DiFazio had perhaps set Giordano up. A Bronx man name Ernesto Rodriguez was allegedly paid $50,000 to carry out the hit.

LATINI, BRUNO

Tenth Avenue and West Forty-ninth Street

On December 25, 1971, the lifeless body of mob associate Bruno Latini was found inside his car in the parking garage at this location. The victim, whose brother was Gambino capo Eddie Lino, had just left a restaurant he owned on Eighth Avenue, only four blocks from the crime scene.

According to *The Ice Man: Confessions of a Mafia Contract Killer* by Philip Carlo, the triggerman was the "Ice Man" himself, Richard Kuklinski—the notorious three-hundred-pound, Polish/Irish American hit man who claimed to have murdered over 250 men on behalf of the New York and New Jersey mob over four decades.

The murder of Latini may have been personal, however. During an interview at Trenton State Prison, Kuklinski allegedly admitted to Carlo

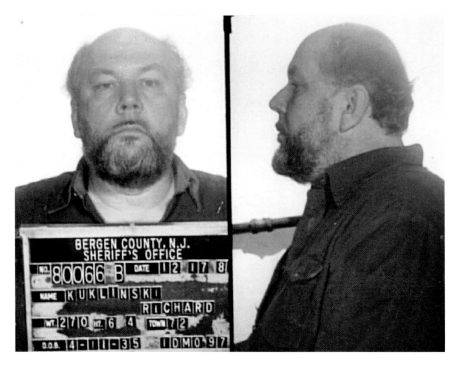

Richard "the Iceman" Kuklinski mug shot, 1986.

that he killed the restaurateur "out of principle." According to the Ice Man, Latini owed him $1,500 and refused to pay, feeling his mob connections would shield him.

After the Kuklinski family celebrated Christmas Eve dinner at their New Jersey home on the night of the murder, Richard snuck out and drove to Manhattan looking for the man who had been avoiding him. He tracked Latini to the parking garage at this location, where the would-be victim was getting into his car. Latini invited Kuklinski into the vehicle to talk about the situation, but when Latini refused to fork over $1,500, the Ice Man pulled out a .38-caliber revolver and shot his victim two times in the head at close range. Kuklinski then took $1,500 from Latini's wallet and returned home to his family; he was never charged with the murder.

Luciano, Charlie
Sixth Avenue and West Fiftieth Street

Charlie Lucky claimed he was abducted at this location on October 17, 1929, by three men who forced him into the backseat of a car, beat him and stabbed him several times in the back. The gangster claims he blacked out after being stabbed and woke up on the side of a road in Staten Island.

Luciano never identified his assailants, and several theories have since emerged, including one that law enforcement agents may have been behind the attack. This theory is based on the fact that no other person in history has ever been "taken for a ride" and lived to tell about it. Some believe the incident was an attempt to either shake up the rising mobster or gain information.

Madonia, Benedetto
743 East Eleventh Street

On the morning of Tuesday, April 14, 1903, the body of Benedetto Madonia, a Sicilian immigrant living in Buffalo, New York, was found stuffed inside of a wooden sugar barrel on the sidewalk in front of this address.

The victim, whose throat was stabbed repeatedly with a stiletto, matched the description of a man that the Secret Service had observed in the company of the Morello gang in the days leading up to the murder. Acting in concert with local authorities, eight Morello gang members were rounded up on April 15 in a coordinated sting—all were armed with revolvers and daggers and put up a fight but were overpowered by police in the vicinity of the Bowery. Four others, including Giuseppe Morello, were picked up soon after and thrown in jail in lieu of a hefty bail. In the pockets of Morello and gang member Tommaso Petto when arrested were cigars of a "peculiar brand," which were also found in the pockets of the victim. This and the testimony of three Secret Service agents was enough to hold the gang on suspicion of murder.

In Petto's possession were a large-caliber revolver and a stiletto that police suspected might have been used in the murder. They also found a pawn

A rare image of Benedetto Madonia (center), two unidentified Morello gang members (left) and gang member Vito Laduca (right). Oakland Tribune, *Oakland, California, May 9, 1903.*

ticket from the Collateral Loan Company at 278 Bowery—for a watch belonging to the victim. When investigated, the broker's description of the person who had pawned the watch matched Petto's; he had purchased the timepiece for one dollar.

Police tried desperately to establish the victim's identity, a motive and a definitive link to the Morellos, whom authorities called "the most dangerous band of counterfeiters that ever operated in this country."[138] Several pieces of evidence were uncovered in Giuseppe's dingy apartment at 178 Christie Street, including a letter written to the gang leader from the victim and another paper with Madonia's name scribbled in red ink—later described as the "signal of death" by the press.[139] The problem was, at the time, authorities did not know who Madonia was.

The cards began to stack up against the Corleone outfit when an identical barrel was found in the 226 Elizabeth Street basement, where police believed the murder occurred. Though the space belonged to the Dolceria

Pasticceria on the first floor, there was no baking equipment on the premises (thus, there seemed to be no need for a full barrel of sugar). In fact, the basement was almost completely empty, and several hidden compartments were found. Since there was still not enough evidence to make a conviction, defense lawyers fought hard to have the gang released. Under mounting pressure, some gang members were dismissed on April 20.

Police caught a break when an anonymous letter they received was investigated, leading them to Giuseppe De Primo, a Morello gang member who was serving time in Sing Sing prison for his role in the 1902 Morristown counterfeiting ring. Famed NYPD detective Joseph Petrosino visited De Primo behind bars on March 21. De Primo told the detective that he had asked Benedetto Madonia, his brother-in-law, to visit New York to try and recover money from the Morello gang, which he felt was owed.

Later that day, Petrosino made a special trip to Buffalo to meet with Madonia's wife (and De Primo's sister), Lucia. She was shown a picture of the deceased and confirmed that it was her husband. Lucia Madonia explained to Petrosino that she and Benedetto were originally from Larcara Fredo, Sicily, near Palermo, and that her husband belonged to a "secret society."[140] She believed that "Giuseppe Morrellio [*sic*]" was part of this society, of which she did not know the name.

The day after Mrs. Madonia was questioned, Giuseppe Morello was taken from his jail cell at the Tombs prison and brought to the morgue in order to examine the mutilated body of the victim. Police hoped the experience would shock Morello into admission, but the steely thirty-six-year-old was unfazed. He was ultimately acquitted on April 23, due to lack of evidence.[141]

Tomasso Petto ended up taking the fall and being charged with the murder of Benedetto Madonia. However, he had somehow slipped out of custody and disappeared, resurfacing a couple years later in Pennsylvania. Petto was never convicted for the murder, and the Morello gang survived the incident relatively intact.

MARANZANO, SALVATORE

230 Park Avenue

Short-lived but influential "boss of all bosses" Salvatore Maranzano (July 31, 1886–September 10, 1931) rose to power during the violent 1930–31 conflict between Sicilian Corleonesi and Castellammare Mafia clans of New York City, in what is known as the Castellammarese War.

Hailing from Castellammare Del Golfo, Maranzano inherited what would become known as the Bonanno crime family in July 1930, after interim boss Vito Bonventre was murdered during the war with Giuseppe Masseria's Corleone organization.

The Brooklyn-based Castellammarese outfit's previous leader, Nicholas Schiro, simply fled the city in 1930, when presented with the choice of fighting Masseria or paying an embarrassingly large tribute. When successor Bonventre was removed from the picture a few months later, forty-five-year-old Maranzano stepped up to the plate and proved to be no pushover.

With the help of young Charlie Luciano and others, the Castellammarese War ended on April 15, 1931, when Masseria was gunned down in a Brooklyn restaurant. Big changes took place in the American Mafia, largely due to the efforts of Salvatore Maranzano. It is believed that this period is when the current hierarchical structure of the Mafia was incorporated, said to be based on Cesar's Roman military. Several contemporary Mafia codes were also established during this time to prevent the inner prejudices and wanton violence that had plagued the Italian organizations for three decades and inhibited the Mafia's full money-generating potential.

During this restructuring, Maranzano officially established the "Five Families" of the New York Mafia and declared himself *capo di tutti capo*.

As progressive as Maranzano was, he was still too restrictive and Old World for the younger, Americanized Mafiosi, who didn't care much about traditional Italian codes and rituals. Most of the Mafia by this time was made up of first-generation Italian Americans or immigrants who had arrived in the United States at a very young age. Growing up in the cradle of America's melting pot, many from this new generation of mobsters did not carry the same prejudices toward non-Italians when it came to business opportunities, nor did they care about seemingly fatuous wars between provinces.

Maranzano sensed that dissent was growing and decided to make a preemptive strike against the person he thought posed the greatest threat to his throne: Charlie Luciano.

Thinking one step ahead, Luciano sent four men disguised as police detectives to Maranzano's office on the ninth floor of this address on September 10, 1931. The four men overpowered the fiesty Maranzano, who fought back but ultimately fell to multiple knife and gunshot wounds. The killers actually passed the man hired to kill Luciano in the hallway on the way out. It was Vincent "Mad Dog" Coll, who was told that there had been a raid and fled.

MASSERIA, GIUSEPPE

82 Second Avenue

On the morning of August 8, 1922, rising boss Giuseppe Masseria was ambushed by two gunmen while leaving his home at 80 Second Avenue. The first few shots barely missed the wiry gang leader, who fled into a shop at this location before returning fire. With bullets depleted, the gunmen ran across Second Avenue to a waiting getaway car on the corner of East Fifth Street.

As the car sped East toward the Bowery, the would-be assassins met a blockade of International Ladies Garment Workers' Union members, who were just let out of a meeting. The speeding car plowed through the crowd and shot randomly as people panicked. Six people were hit, and two were killed. The gunmen sped away.

Investigating police found Masseria in his apartment totally unscathed, except for two bullet holes through his straw hat.

MORELLO, GIUSEPPE

352 East 116ᵗʰ Street

Sentenced to a twenty-five-year prison term in 1910 for counterfeiting, La Cosa Nostra patriarch Giuseppe Morello's term was commuted, and he

352 East 116th Street today. *Courtesy of Shirley Dluginski.*

was released only a decade later, in 1920. Morello looked to reestablish his position at the top of the Mafia food chain. However, by this time, the game had changed dramatically, and those in power had no intention of turning over their operations. Eventually, Morello may have decided that if he couldn't beat them, he would join them, and he allied himself with Giuseppe Masseria.

On August 15, 1930, Morello, now going by the name "Peter," became one of the first victims of the Castellammarese War. Masseria's new adviser was gunned down in his office on the second floor of this address when two unidentified men burst through the door. He was shot five times and died on the scene. Associate Joseph Perriano leaped out the window with a bullet wound to the chest and died before paramedics could arrive. Another man, Gaspari Pollaro, survived the attack but was in critical condition. The killers were never identified.

PERSICO, ALPHONSE

320 East Seventy-ninth Street

On April 11, 1972, just four days after the murder of "Crazy" Joey Gallo, Alphonse "Little Allie" Persico (older brother of Colombo family boss Carmine Persico), his son and a bodyguard stepped into the former Neapolitan Noodle restaurant at this address for a meal. While the party waited at the bar for a table, a man in a shoulder-length black wig walked in behind them, ordered a scotch and water and threw a ten-dollar bill on the bar.

After a few sips, the man pulled out two pistols, sprung around and began firing in the direction of where Persico had been standing—only by that time, two innocent businessmen named Sheldon Epstein and Max Tekelch had taken the gangster's place. They were both killed in a hail of nine bullets, while Persico and his party were safely seated in the back dining room. The gunman escaped in a getaway car.

This was at least the fifteenth gangland slaying in New York City in the fourteen months since Joe Colombo was shot in Columbus Circle.

SCHIFF, IRWIN

1452 Second Avenue, between 75th and 76th Streets

On the evening of August 8, 1987, 350-pound multimillionaire businessman Irwin "Fat Man" Schiff was dining with a group of twenty friends at the Bravo Sergio Restaurant at this address, when a man in a dark suit casually walked in through a side door and approached Fat Man, firing two bullets into the victim's head before fleeing from the scene. Speculation about a mob connection immediately grew, though investigators initially had a tough time even figuring out who Schiff was.

As the case developed, a story unfolded that grabbed headlines for several weeks. It turned out that the fifty-year-old victim, who had no verifiable income, led quite an extravagant life. He drove antique Rolls-Royces, owned a $500,000 speedboat, lived in a $13,000-a-month penthouse at 415 East Fifty-fourth Street, dated beautiful models and mingled with celebrities at the finest restaurants, casinos, hotels and nightclubs in the world.

On paper, Schiff was the president of the Queens-based Construction Coordinators Corporation. However, that company had neither a telephone number nor an office. It was incorporated in 1984 using a post office box.[142]

Authorities eventually linked Schiff to $70 million in illegal financial transactions. He was convicted of writing fraudulent checks in 1962 and pleaded guilty to tax evasion in 1977. As witnesses came forward and tips began to pour in, speculation grew about Schiff being a mob loan shark. Eventually, a link was established between Schiff and mob boss Louis "Bobby" Manna, who allegedly ran a New Jersey–based Genovese crime family at the time.

Only two days after the murder, FBI surveillance at Casella's Restaurant in Hoboken, New Jersey—former headquarters of the Manna crew—picked up a conversation between retired Hoboken police officer Frank "Dipsy" Daniello and Martin Casella, restaurant owner and Manna lieutenant. In the tapes, the pair was overheard discussing the murder. Daniello said of the gunman, "It takes guts though to do it like that. This kid is a—" Casella interrupted, "Stone killer."[143]

Three days before the murder, another conversation was recorded between two unidentified patrons of Casella's Italian Restaurant. One man asked, "You wanna hit him?" A second man replied, "We'll do him good at night. Bobby Manna didn't like CC." According to the government, "CC" was the mob's code name for Irwin Schiff.

FBI surveillance also picked up a conversation between Casella and Manna himself, plotting to kill Gambino boss John Gotti Sr. and his brother, Gene Gotti. "You know, this should be good and fast if it's John Gotti," Manna was heard saying.[144]

The feds allegedly warned Gotti of the assassination plot and eventually rounded up Manna (who had an apartment at 130 West Houston Street), Casella and four associates, charging them with extortion, loan-sharking, labor racketeering and murder.

Michael Chertoff, then first assistant United States attorney for New Jersey, claimed that Manna, who was described as the third-ranking member of the Genovese crime family, planned the killing of Irwin Schiff, and associate Richard "Bocci" DeSciscio was the man who pulled the trigger.

A lengthy fifteen-week trial began on March 7, 1989. On April 17, a legal secretary who lived above the Bravo Sergio Restaurant bravely picked forty-two-year-old DeSciscio out from the witness stand and placed him at the scene of the murder. Over the next two months, several witnesses took the stand, including Genovese soldier turned state's witness Vincent "Fish" Cafaro and the thirty-three-year-old blond model with whom Schiff was dining on the night of the murder.

On June 26, 1989, Mana, Casella and DeSciscio were convicted of murder and the conspiracy to assassinate the Gotti brothers. Three others were convicted of various racketeering and conspiracy charges. On September 26, 1989, Manna and Casella were sentenced to eighty years behind bars, while DeSciscio received a seventy-five-year sentence—essentially life in prison, since none of the defendants is eligible for parole until 2049.

During the trial, it was discovered that Schiff had received at least $10 million in payments from the Luis Electric Contracting Corporation of Long Island City, Queens, which had secured more than $50 million in sweetheart public contracts in just a decade—including a $10 million deal to wire the new Jacob Javits Convention Center (655 West Thirty-fourth Street) in the late 1970s.

An exact motive for the killing of Irwin "Fat Man" Schiff is unclear to this day, though in August 1987, federal law enforcement officials claimed that Schiff was leading a double life by working as an FBI informant.[145]

SLIWA, CURTIS

113 Avenue A

In the early morning of June 19, 1992, the high-profile leader of the Guardian Angels was on his way to work at WABC radio in Midtown, where he hosted a talk show, when he exited Ray's Candy Store at this address and jumped into the backseat of a cab. As the taxi began to speed off, a man hiding in the front seat popped up and opened fire on Sliwa, who managed to tumble out of the moving vehicle about a block away with bullet wounds to his leg and groin.

This brazen attack on Curtis Sliwa (March 26, 1954–) was the second in as many months. A cast from the thirty-eight-year-old's broken wrist had just been removed; the wrist injury was sustained in a baseball bat assault on April 23 at the same location.

A turncoat Gambino soldier named Joseph D'Angelo later confessed to being the driver of the cab and implicated that John Gotti Jr. was behind the assault; however, three separate juries were unable to find Gotti guilty, and he was acquitted.

As of this writing, John Gotti Jr. is involved in the production of a movie based on his famous family, and Curtis Sliwa, who founded the Guardian Angels citizen patrol group in 1979, has a new battle on his hands. The veteran crime fighter is protesting the making of the Gotti movie.

TERRANOVA, VINCENZO

2nd Avenue and 116th Street

The youngest Terranova brother met his end at this location on May 8, 1922, when a shotgun blast from a moving vehicle left the veteran gangster in a pool of blood on the sidewalk. Terranova managed to fire several shots at his assassins as they sped away before dying of his injuries at the scene.

It is believed that Rocco Valenti was responsible for the murder, which kicked off a bloody three-month war between the D'Aquila and Masseria clans.

TRESCA, CARLO

Fifth Avenue at West Sixteenth Street (Lower West Side)

Carlo Tresca was the editor of a popular Italian-language, anti-Fascist newspaper called *Il Martello* (The Hammer), which was published at 208 East Twelfth Street.

On January 11, 1943, at 9:40 p.m., Tresca was walking near this intersection when an unidentified man approached and shot him to death. The assailant jumped into a Ford sedan (New York license plate number 1C9272, for the record), where two other men were waiting, and fled the scene.

Several theories surrounding this unsolved murder lead back to Carmine Galante, though none could ever be proven. One theory claims that Vito Genovese hired Frank Garafolo to arrange the assassination as a favor to Italian dictator Umberto Mussolini. Another theory suggests that Tresca offended Garafolo at a dinner event on September 10, 1942, and ordered the hit himself.

Galante was initially connected to the crime because he visited his parole officer the same day Tresca was killed—in the same automobile the murderers used in their getaway. He was arrested three days later, but lack of evidence prevented his prosecution.

Valenti, Umberto "Rocco"

East Twelfth Street at Second Avenue

On August 11, 1922, just three days after a failed hit on Giuseppe Masseria outside 82 Second Avenue, Valenti was invited to a "sidewalk meeting" on the busy corner of East Twelfth Street and Second Avenue, just steps from John's Restaurant, under the veil of a peace talk.

When Valenti arrived at the meeting with two bodyguards at about 11:45 a.m., he was greeted by a half dozen gunmen. Under a barrage of bullets, an eight-year-old girl and a street cleaner were wounded. As Valenti tried to jump onto a moving taxi to escape, he was shot and killed. Gangland legend says the gunman was future crime boss Charlie Luciano.

Verrazano, Giuseppe

341 Broome Street

On October 5, 1916, two men walked into the Italian Garden Restaurant located on the first floor of this address and opened fire on Morello gang member Giuseppe Verrazano. Another gunman stood guard at the door in case their victim tried to flee, but it was not necessary. Verrazano was killed at his table.

Verrazano was originally set up to be killed alongside Nicolas Morello and "Charles" Ubriaco during an ambush in Brooklyn on September 7, 1916, but he did not make the trip for some reason, so Neapolitan crime boss Pellegrino Morano sent his men after the Sicilian a month later to finish the job.

Morano was later convicted of the September 7 murders of Morello and Ubriaco and deported back to Italy by 1919.

WOLOSKY, DAVID

Northwest Corner of First Avenue and East Sixteenth Street

The body of bookie and ex-con David Wolosky, also known as David Kaye, was found by a beat cop at this location at about 1:30 a.m. on April 19, 1972. He had been shot three times in the back elsewhere and dropped off in front of the Beth Israel Hospital on this corner.

In Wolosky's pockets were three sets of identification, several gambling slips and some loose change. He had at least ten prior arrests, including felonious assault and grand larceny.

It was the city's eighth gangland slaying and umpteenth shooting in three weeks—including the Joey Gallo murder on April 7. Just the night before Wolosky was murdered, Thomas Graziano (nephew of the legendary boxer) had been shot in the abdomen at First Avenue and East Twelfth Street. He survived.

APPENDIX
MAPS AND CHARTS

Included here are some materials to give a better sense of the stories in this book and help you navigate through the primary neighborhood's discussed.

	GENOVESE	GAMBINO	BONANNO	LUCCHESE	COLOMBO
1931 BOSS:	Charlie Luciano	Vincent Mangano	Joe Bonanno	Tommy Gagliano	Joseph Profaci
1931 UNDERBOSS:	Vito Genovese	Albert Anastasia	John Bonventre	Tommy Lucchese	Joe Magliocco
1931 CONSIGLIERE:	Frank Costello	Philip Mangano	John Tartamella	Stefano Rondelli	Salvatore Profaci
OTHER BOSSES:	Costello, Genovese, Vincent Gigante	Anastasia, Carlo Gambino, Paul Castellano, John Gotti	Salvatore Maranzano, Natale Evola, Carmine Gigante	Lucchese, Anthony Corallo	Joe Colombo
ORIGINS:	Giuseppe Masseria's Prohibition era crime outfit, which itself was an incarnate of Giuseppe Morello's turn of century gang.	Salvatore D'Aquila's early century crime family with roots in East Harlem.	Nicola Schiro's Brooklyn-based Castellammarese family, itself an incarnate of Giuseppe Bonanno's (Joe's uncle) turn of century outfit.	Gaetano Reina's 1920s outfit based in East Harlem and the Bronx.	When Salvatore D'Aquila was killed in 1928, some of his Brooklyn-based rackets were awarded to Profaci and a fifth "Family" was born.

New York's "Five Families," officially christened in 1931. *Lower East Side History Project.*

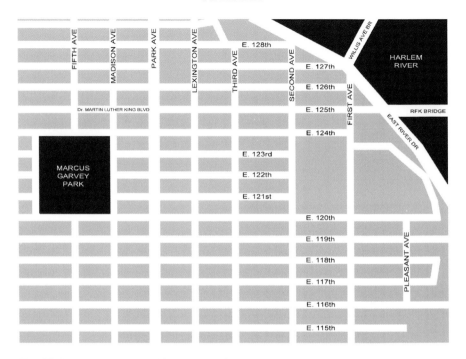

East Harlem map. *Lower East Side History Project.*

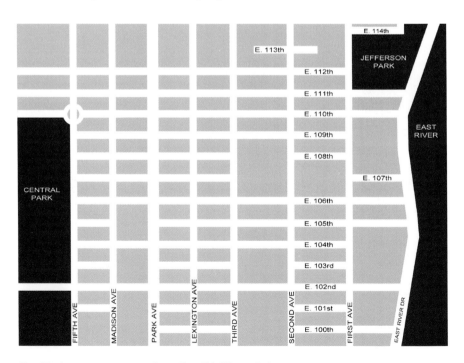

East Harlem map, part two. *Lower East Side History Project.*

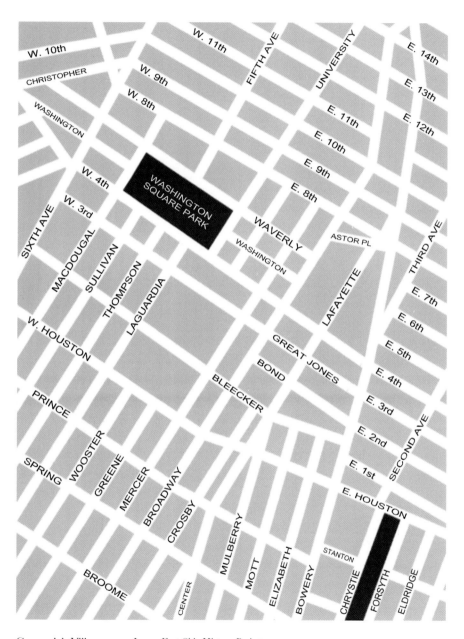

Greenwich Village map. *Lower East Side History Project.*

East Village map. *Lower East Side History Project.*

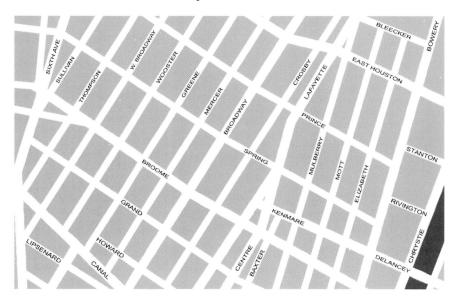

Little Italy map. *Lower East Side History Project*.

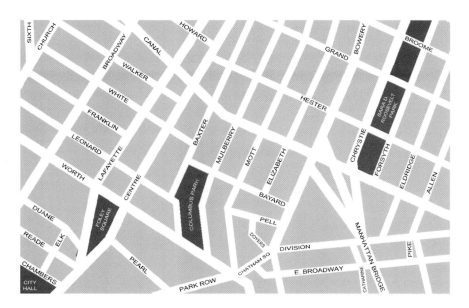

Little Italy map, part two. *Lower East Side History Project*.

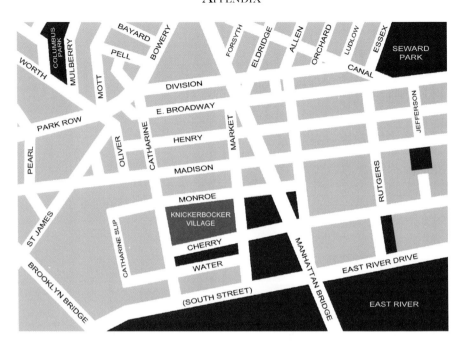

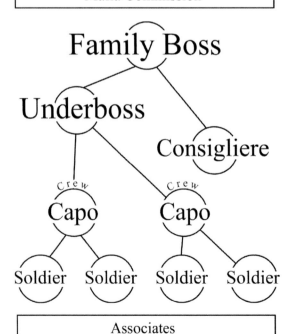

Above: Fourth Ward, Lower East Side map. *Lower East Side History Project*.

Left: Structure of a Mafia family. *Lower East Side History Project*.

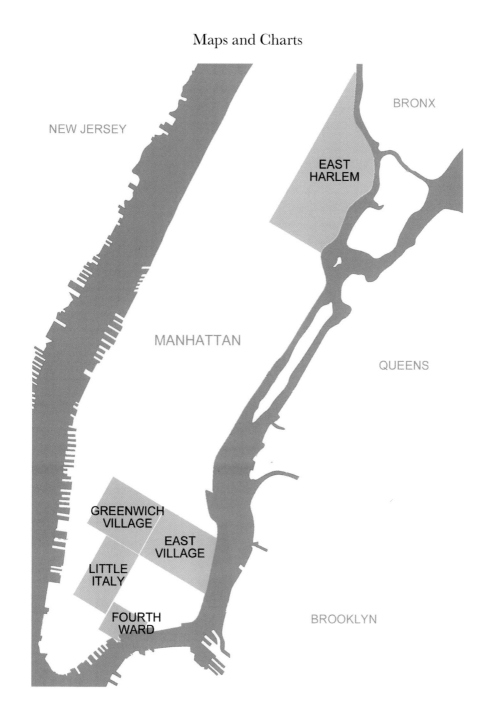

Districts of Manhattan primarily discussed in this book. *Lower East Side History Project*.

NOTES

PREFACE

1. *New York Times*, "Must Stop Outrages by the Black Hand," January 26, 1908.
2. *Tri City Herald* [Richland, WA], "Valachi Testimony Rated Best Show on TV Network," October 2, 1963.

I. PROFILES

3. Some sources list Attardi's birth as September 12, 1900, or April 1, 1892, and death as July 17, 1970.
4. FBN memo dated December 13, 1938, NARA Record Number 124-90093-10099.
5. According to the FBN, Attardi frequented "159 Christie Street near Delancey." This could be the address to his shop.
6. Feder and Joesten, *Luciano Story*.
7. Messick, *John Edgar Hoover*.
8. *United States of America, Respondent-Appellee v. Angelo Buia, Defendant-Appellant.*, 236 F.2d 548 (2nd Cir. 1956).
9. *New York Times*, "11 Seized in Raid on Narcotics Ring," August 10, 1962.
10. United States Congress, *Organized Crime*.
11. *New York Times*, "4 Get Prison Terms in Narcotics Cases," October 5, 1955.

12. Phil Sanford, "The Inside Story," *Miami News*, April 11, 1980.

13. Dannen, *Hit Men*.

14. Cole and Hinckley, *Sh-Boom!*.

15. Rose, *The Agency*.

16. *New York Times*, "Six Indicted in Conspiracy To Sell Stolen Securities," April 12, 1968.

17. United States Federal Narcotics Control Board, *Traffic in Opium*.

18. Lawrence O'Kane, "11 Seized in Raid on Narcotics Ring," *New York Times*, August 10, 1962.

19. *West's Federal Supplement*. Vol. 842. West Publishing Company, 1994.

20. Jacobs and Daniels, *Friend of the Family*.

21. *Toledo* [Ohio] *Blade*, "Alleged Crime Bosses Seized in New York Police Raid," September 23, 1966.

22. *New York Times*, "Hentel Accused on Arrest of 13," December 20, 1966.

23. Though spelled with a "t" in the following article, this could be Genovese family soldier Joseph Tortorici.

24. *New York Evening Post*, "Schultz Gang Aid Held in Club Raid," January 7, 1936.

25. *United States of America, Appellee v. Joseph D'Ercole and Marty Russo, Defendant-Appellants*, 225 F.2d 611 (2nd Cir. 1955).

26. *Joseph D'Ercole, Appellant v. United States of America, Appellee*, 361 F.2d 211 (2nd Cir. 1966).

27. Nash, A., *New York City Gangland*.

28. *New York Times*, "Cosa Nostra Aides Cleared by Court In Consorting Case," November 4, 1965.

29. United States Congress House Subcommittee, *Departments of State*.

30. *Los Angeles Times*, "Top Mafia Leadership Listed by Justice Dept.," August 22, 1969.

31. Nicholas Pileggi, "Gangbusters," *New York Magazine*, July 25, 1983.

32. *New York Times*, "Murder in Brooklyn Is Laid to Gangsters," August 5, 1930.

33. Dr. Anthony Baltakis, *Kennedy Assassination Chronicles*, Vol. 5, Issue 1, Politics and Policies of JFK and RFK: The McClellan Committee Investigation of Organized Labor, 1998.

34. Sam Baron, "A Top Teamster Fights Back," *Life*, July 20, 1962.

35. *United States of America, Appellee v. Domenico Bando, A/K/a 'Nick Bando,' Leo Telvi and Gondolfo Miranti, A/K/A 'Shiekie,' Appellants*, 244 F.2d 833 (2nd Cir. 1957).

36. Fed. Sec. L. Rep. P 94,534 *United States of America, Appellee v. John Dioguardi and Louis Ostrer, Defendants-Appellants.*, 492 F.2d 70 (2nd Cir. 1974).

37. *John Dioguardi, Petitioner-Appellant v. United States of America, Respondent-Appellee*, 587 F.2d 572 (2nd Cir. 1978).

38. *United States of America, Appellee v. Harry Stromberg, Henry Teitelbaum, Jean Aron, Nathan Behrman, Martin de Saverio, George Brisbois, Herman Samnick, Benjamin Danis, Saul Snyder, Salvatore Maimone, Anthony Mirra, Steve Puco, Daniel Lessa, Nicholas Lessa and Leo Seto, Defendants-Appellants*, 268 F.2d 256 (2nd Cir. 1959).

39. *United States of America, Appellee v. Alfredo Aviles, Charles Barcellona, Jean Capece, Charles Di Palermo, Joseph Di Palermo, Natale Evola, Vito Genovese, Vincent Gigante, Daniel Lessa, Nicholas Lessa, Rocco Mazzie, Carmine Polizzano, Ralph Polizzano, Benjamin Rodriquez, and Salvatore Santora, Appellants*, 274 F.2d 179 (2nd Cir. 1960).

40. *United States of America, Appellee v. Peter Di Palermo, Appellant*, 228 F.2d 901 (2nd Cir. 1956).

41. The FBN lists Di Pietro's death as 1978, though reliable sources claim he was killed in the 1980s, possibly at the hands of a Gambino gunman.

42. Nicholas Pileggi, "The Story of T," *New York Times Magazine*, March 29, 1970.

43. *United States of America, Appellee v. William Bentvena Et Al., Defendants-Appellants*, 319 F.2d 916 (2nd Cir. 1963).

44. Many sources claim Embarrato was born in New York City on November 1, 1909, as "Alfred James Embarrato"; however, several original source documents such as census records, a ship manifest and petition for U.S. citizenship under the name "Alfred Joseph Embarrato" contradict this. Embarrato himself claimed he was born in Italy on November 12 in these documents.

45. *United States of America, Plaintiff-Appellee v. Alfred Embarrato, Defendant-Appellant*, 253 F.2d 947 (2nd Cir. 1958).

46. *United States of America, Plaintiff-Appellant v. the Bonanno Organized Crime Family of La Cosa Nostra*, 879 F.2d 20 (2nd Cir. 1989).

47. Kevin McCoy, "Tapes Bare Mob Hold on Post," *New York Newsday*, July 23, 1992.

48. John Marzulli, "Former Post Exec Marries Paper to Mob," *New York Post*, June 11, 2004.
49. *United States of America, Appellee v. Russell A. Bufalino, Ignatius Cannone, Paul C. Castellano, Joseph F. Civello, Frank A. Desimone, Natale Evola, Louis A. Larasso, Carmine Lombardozzi, Joseph Magliocco, Frank T. Majuri, Michele Miranda, John C. Montana, John Ormento, James Osticco, Joseph Profaci, Anthony P. Riela, John T. Scalish, Angelo J. Sciandra, Simone Scozzari and Pasquale Turrigiano, Defendants-Appellants*, 285 F.2d 408 (2ⁿᵈ Cir. 1960).
50. *United States of America, Appellee v. Alfredo Aviles, Charles Barcellona, Jean Capece, Charles Di Palermo, Joseph Di Palermo, Natale Evola, Vito Genovese, Vincent Gigante, Daniel Lessa, Nicholas Lessa, Rocco Mazzie, Carmine Polizzano, Ralph Polizzano, Benjamin Rodriquez, and Salvatore Santora, Appellants*, 274 F.2d 179 (2ⁿᵈ Cir. 1960).
51. *United States of America, Appellee v. Joseph Morello and Rosario Farulla, Defendants-Appellants*, 250 F.2d 631 (2ⁿᵈ Cir. 1957).
52. Unites States Congress, *Hearings*, Vol. 18, 201.
53. Harvey Klehr, "All the Right Enemies: The Life and Murder of Carlo Tresca," *Washington Monthly* 20 (November 10, 1888).
54. Some historians and insiders believe this summit never took place. According to Mafioso turned informer Tommaso Buscetta, Charlie Luciano simply hosted a dinner in honor of Joseph Bonanno at the hotel, which was attended by a handful of close associates. Authorities tracking Luciano's movements at the time reported on the meetings, but those reports were buried until the 1965 investigation.
55. *Deseret News* [Utah], "Italy Police Round Up 14 Leaders in Mafia," August 2, 1965.
56. *New York Times*, "8 Indicted in Brooklyn as Counterfeiters," June 20, 1930.
57. *Herald-Journal* [Spartanburg, SC], "Today," September 21, 1934.
58. *New York Times*, "Poisoning Threat in Jail Revealed," November 20, 1945.
59. James Miller, "The People Vs.," *Life*, August 30, 1968.
60. *United States of America, Appellee v. Joseph Gernie and Edward Ogull, Defendants-Appellants*, 252 F.2d 664 (2ⁿᵈ Cir. 1958).
61. *Gadsden Times* [Alabama], "Vincent Gigante Back to Truck," May 28, 1958.
62. *New York Times*, "Genovese is Given 15 Years in Prison in Narcotics Ring," April 18, 1959.

63. Selwyn Raab, "Vincent Gigante, Mafia Leader Who Feigned Insanity, Dies at 77," *New York Times*, December 19, 2005.

64. Collins, *Newswalker.*

65. Chris Wall, "Bright Lights," *Sunday Herald*, February 17, 1952.

66. *New York Times*, "Ianniello Is Sentenced In Racketeering Trial," February 16, 1986.

67. *New York Times*, "U.S. Attorney Reports Indictment of Ianniello," May 16, 1986.

68. Sports Section, *Bridgeport* [CT] *Sunday Herald*, October 3, 1897.

69. Alfred Emanuel Smith and Francis Walton, "The Street Gang as a Factor in Politics," *New Outlook* 74 (May 2, 1903).

70. *St. John Daily Sun* [New Brunswick, Canada], "Wickedest Child in New York a Girl. Depravity Unbelievable," September 26, 1903.

71. *New York Times*, "Two Policemen Beaten," July 24, 1901

72. *World* [New York], "City Officialy Warned Jerome of the Plot," October 30, 1901.

73. *New York Times*, "Seth Low's Busy Evening," November 2, 1901.

74. *New York Times*, "Peace Marks Devery's Association Outing," September 11, 1902.

75. *New York Times*, "Rival Bands Battle in Chinatown Streets," September 30, 1902.

76. *New York Times*, "Battle in a Poolroom," October 5, 1902.

77. *New York Times*, "Leader Foley Settles Feud," October 12, 1902.

78. *New York Times*, "Picnickers Fight Police," July 6, 1903.

79. *New York Times*, "Policemen Fight a Mob," July 9, 1903.

80. *World* [New York], "They Spoil Faces," October 24, 1903.

81. *New York Times*, "Shields Man Who Shot Him," March 14, 1904.

82. *New York Times*, "Fought Detectives on Roof," November 14, 1904.

83. *New York Times*, "Eat 'Em Up Jack McManus Killed in Feud," May 27, 1905.

84. *St. John Daily Sun* [New Brunswick, Canada], "Former St. John Bartender Murdered in Bowery Row," June 3, 1905

85. *Sun* [Baltimore, MD], "Complete Paralysis of New York Harbor Threatened," April 19, 1919.

86. *New York Times*, "Vaccarelli to Play Drum to Join Union," January 25, 1923.

87. *New York Times*, "2 DROWN OFF PIER, HAD DRUNK ALCOHOL; Two Others, Who Had Also Fallen In after Swallowing Mixture, Are Saved," August 10, 1924.

88. Lanza was not president of the USW, as is often cited.

89. *New York Times*, "DEFIANCE OF GANGS TOLD," April 11, 1931.

90. *Day* [New London, CT], "Fulton Fish Market Confusion Is Invitation to Racketeer Methods," December 12, 1931.

91. *Report of Violation of Parole*, New York State Division of Parole, April 11, 1957.

92. Lisi is often misidentified as a member of the Lucchese family.

93. Several sources cite Lisi's mother's name as "Nellie," which is semicorrect. Though she arrived in America under the name "Sebartiana Grno," her first name appears as "Neli" on several documents, including a 1927 naturalization petition. However, by 1942, records show that she was using the spelling "Nellie."

94. In the 1950s, veteran mobster Joe Profaci admitted during an INS examination that when first arriving in America, he had visited Antonio Lucania (when Luciano was still a young boy), though he did not elaborate on the nature of the visit and denied any relationship, business or otherwise, with the Mafia icon.

95. Bernstein, *Greatest Menace*.

96. *New York Times*, "LUCANIA IS CALLED SHALLOW PARASITE," June 19, 1936

97. *Calgary Herald*, "Luciano Role Brings Actor Death Threats," February 26, 1962

98. The FBN cites Mari's birth as September 3, 1926; however, other documents, including his death index, state he was born on July 27.

99. *New York Times*, "Club Pleads Guilty," May 22, 1957.

100. *Anthony Mirra, Petitioner-Appellant v. United States of America, Respondent-Appellee*, 379 F.2d 782 (2nd Cir. 1967).

101. *New York Times*, "13 Are Sentenced in Narcotics Case," July 11, 1962.

102. *New York Times*, "A Nightclub Owner Says He Has Woes—The Mafia," October 10, 1974.

103. According to Dash, *First Family*, Bernardo Terranova lived at 123 East Fourth Street as late as 1900.

104. His last name was actually Lupo; it was not a nickname as is regularly reported. His father's last name was Lupo, and his mother's maiden name was Saietta.

105. *New York Times,* "Black Hand Block Raided by Flynn," January 8, 1911.

106. Several sources, including the FBN, cite Petillo's mother as "Mary Lomberdi"; however, original source documents, like census records and passport applications, contradict this.

107. Federal Bureau of Investigation FOIA report on David Petillo.

108. *Asbury* [NJ] *Park Press,* "Mobster Living in Home Owned by a Police Chief," January 9, 1975.

109. *United States of America, Appellee v. Alfredo Aviles, Charles Barcellona, Jean Capece, Charles Di Palermo, Joseph Di Palermo, Natale Evola, Vito Genovese, Vincent Gigante, Daniel Lessa, Nicholas Lessa, Rocco Mazzie, Carmine Polizzano, Ralph Polizzano, Benjamin Rodriquez, and Salvatore Santora, Appellants,* 274 F.2d 179 (2nd Cir. 1960).

110. *United States of America, Appellee v. Giacomo Reina, Joseph Valachi, Pasquale Moccio, Pasquale Pagano and Larry Quartiero, Appellants,* 242 F.2d 302 (2nd Cir. 1957).

111. *Syracuse* [NY] *Herald Journal,* "Harness Race Fixing Charges Dismissed," October 28, 1983.

112. *Time,* "Crime: Most Damnably Outrageous," August 10, 1931.

113. *New York Times,* "COSTELLO ON LIST OF 150 RACKETEERS IN U.S. CRIME QUEST," May 9, 1950.

114. *New York Times,* "Five Get Long Terms in Narcotics Cases," November 30, 1954.

115. *Idaho State Journal,* "Luciano Linked to Crime Play," July 1, 1968.

116. *Corpus Christi* [TX] *Times,* "17 Top Mafia-Cosa Nostra Bosses on Trial in Sicily," March 14, 1968.

117. *New York Times,* "Two Men Held As Robbers," March 22, 1926.

118. *Telegraph-Herald* [IA], "Blonde Dancer Plunges to Death," April 19, 1938.

119. *Portsmouth* [OH] *Times,* "Holdup Heroin Leaps to Death; Blow Blamed," April 15, 1938.

120. *Youngstown* [OH] *Vindicator,* "Crime City Racketeer Found Beaten on the Docks," July 6, 1952.

121. *Reading* [PA] *Eagle,* "Valachi Puts Finger on Vito Genovese as Crime Overlord," September 27, 1963.

122. *Chicago Daily Tribune,* "Names Chicago Gangsters Who Face Tax Quiz," March 21, 1951.

123. Tuminaro may have been born on February 22, 1909.

124. Valentine, *Strength of the Wolf.*

125. Ibid.

126. Internal FBI files on the JFK assassination, written August 23, 1968, released October 3, 1996 (NARA Record Number: 124-10288-10422).

II. Social Clubs and Hangouts

127. Cole and Hinckley, *Sh-Boom!.*

128. *Indiana* [PA] *Gazette*, "New Yorkers' $12 Billion Gambling Tab Tops in Nation," February 14, 1993.

129. Breslin, *Good Rat.*

130. Bonanno, Pistone and Fisher, *Good Guys.*

III. Gangland Hits

131. *Bulletin* [Bend, OR], "Gunman's Poor Aim Saves Defendant," February 15, 1987.

132. *Chicago Tribune*, "Mafia Case Witness to Tell More," December 24, 1987.

133. *New York Times*, "Shot by Shot, an Ex-Aide to Gotti Describes the Killing of Castellano," March 4, 1992.

134. *Times Daily* [Florence, AL], "Vincent Coll Gets His Lead From Gangdom," February 8, 1932.

135. *New York Times*, "Three Slay Man in Street and Flee," October 11, 1928.

136. *New York Post*, "Mafia's Whacks & Pacts," February 8, 2008.

137. *New York Times*, "Ex-Assistant Prosecutor for Hogan Shot to Death in 'Village' Ambush," November 5, 1977.

138. *New York Times*, "Eight Sicilians Held For Barrel Murder," April 16, 1903.

139. *Meriden* [CT] *Daily Journal*, "Mafia Leader Iron-Nerved," April 23, 1903.

140. *Nashua* [NH] *Daily Telegraph*, "From Buffalo," April 21, 1903.

141. *Boston Evening Transcript*, "Suspected Italian Discharged," April 22, 1903.

142. *Pittsburgh Press*, "Slaying Opens Mystery of Man's True Identity," August 16, 1987.

143. *New York Times*, "Tapes Tell How Schiff Was Murdered," April 16, 1989.

144. *New York Times*, "TAPED MEETINGS DETAIL MOB PLOT TO KILL 2 GOTTIS," July 2, 1988.

145. *New York Newsday*, "Schiff, Victim of `Crime Hit,' Described as FBI Informant," August 12, 1987.

BIBLIOGRAPHY

Bernstein, Lee Adam. *The Greatest Menace: Organized Crime in United States Culture and Politics, 1946–1961.* N.p.: University of Minnesota, 1997.

Bonanno, Bill, Joe Piston and David Fisher. *The Good Guys.* N.p.: Hachette Digital, Inc., 2005.

Breslin, Jimmy. *The Good Rat: A True Story.* New York: HarperCollins, 2009.

Cannistraro, Philip V., and Gerald Meyer. *The Lost World of Italian American Radicalism: Politics, Labor, and Culture.* Westport, CT: Greenwood Publishing Group, 2003.

Capeci, Jerry. *Jerry Capeci's Gang Land.* New York: Penguin, 2003.

Carlo, Philip. *The Ice Man: Confessions of a Mafia Contract Killer.* New York: Macmillan, 2009.

Cole, Clay, and David Hinckley. *Sh-Boom!: The Explosion of Rock 'n' Roll (1953–1968).* Bloomington, IN: Wordclay, 2009.

Collins, R. Thomas. *Newswalker: A Story for Sweeney.* Fairfax, VA: RavensYard Publishing, Ltd., 2002.

Critchley, David. *The Origin of Organized Crime in America: The New York City Mafia, 1891–1931.* London: Taylor & Francis U.S., 2009.

Dannen, Fredric. *Hit Men: Power Brokers and Fast Money Inside the Music Business.* New York: Vintage Books, 1991.

Dash, Mike. *The First Family: Terror, Extortion, Revenge, Murder and the Birth of the American Mafia.* New York: Random House, 2010.

Davis, John H. *Mafia Dynasty: The Rise and Fall of the Gambino Crime Family.* New York: HarperCollins, 1994.

Dickie, John. *Cosa Nostra: A History of the Sicilian Mafia*. New York: Macmillan, 2005.

Feder, Sid, and Joachim Joesten. *The Luciano Story*. New York: Da Capo Press, 1994.

Fijnaut, Cyrille, and James B. Jacobs. *Organized Crime and Its Containment: A Transatlantic Initiative*. Leiden, Netherlands: Martinus Nijhoff Publishers, 1991.

Gambetta, Diego. *The Sicilian Mafia: The Business of Private Protection*. Cambridge, MA: Harvard University Press, 1996.

Giancana, Sam, and Bureau of Narcotics, United States Treasury Department. *Mafia: The Government's Secret File on Organized Crime*. New York: Skyhorse Publishing Inc., 2009.

Harrell, G.T. *For Members Only: The Story of the Mob's Secret Judge*. Bloomington, IN: AuthorHouse, 2008.

Hill, Henry, and Bryon Schreckengost. *A Goodfella's Guide to New York: Your Personal Tour Through the Mob's Notorious Haunts, Hair-Raising Crime Scenes, and Infamous Hot Spots*. New York: Random House, 2003.

Jacobs, D. Lea, and Anthony Daniels. *Friend of the Family: An Undercover Agent in the Mafia*. Washington, D.C.: Howells House, 2002.

Jacobs, James B., Christopher Panarella and Jay Worthington. *Busting the Mob: United States v. Cosa Nostra*. New York: New York University Press, 1996.

Marrs, Jim. *Crossfire: The Plot That Killed Kennedy*. New York: Basic Books, 1990.

Messick, Hank. *John Edgar Hoover: An Inquiry into the Life and Times of John Edgar Hoover, and His Relationship to the Continuing Partnership of Crime, Business, and Politics*. N.p.: McKay, 1972.

Moore, Robin. *The French Connection: A True Account of Cops, Narcotics, and International Conspiracy*. Guilford, CT: Globe Pequot, 2003.

Mustain, Gene, and Jerry Capeci. *Mob Star: The Story of John Gotti*. New York: Penguin, 2002.

Nash, Arthur. *New York City Gangland*. Mount Pleasant, SC: Arcadia Publishing, 2010.

Nash, Jay Robert. *Encyclopedia of World Crime: D-J*. Wilmette, IL: CrimeBooks, 1990.

National Trades and Workers Association (U.S.) and Citizens' Industrial Association of America. *The Square Deal*. Vol. 5. New York: Citizens' Industrial Association of America, 1908.

Pernicone, Nunzio. *Carlo Tresca: Portrait of a Rebel.* New York: Macmillan, 2005.

Pistone, Joseph. *Way of the Wiseguy.* Philadelphia, PA: Running Press, 2005.

Pistone, Joseph, and Richard Woodley. *Donnie Brasco: My Undercover Life in the Mafia.* New York: Penguin, 1997.

Raab, Selwyn. *Five Families: The Rise, Decline, and Resurgence of America's Most Powerful Mafia Empires.* New York: Macmillan, 2006.

Reppetto, Thomas. *Bringing Down the Mob: The War Against the American Mafia.* New York: Macmillan, 2007.

Rose, Frank. *The Agency: William Morris and the Hidden History of Show Business.* Frank Rose, 1996.

Seindal, René. *Mafia: Money and Politics in Sicily, 1950–1997.* Copenhagen, Denmark: Museum Tusculanum Press, 1998.

Sharman, Russell Leigh. *The Tenants of East Harlem.* Berkeley: University of California Press, 2006.

Sifakis, Carl. *The Mafia Encyclopedia.* New York: Infobase Publishing, 2005.

Smith, John L. *Running Scared: The Life and Treacherous Times of Las Vegas Casino King Steve Wynn.* Cambridge, MA: Da Capo Press, 2001.

United States Congress House Subcommittee on Departments of State. *Departments of State, Justice, and Commerce, the Judiciary, and Related Agencies Appropriations for 1971: Hearings, Ninety-first Congress, Second Session.* Vol. 1. Washington, D.C.: United States Congress, 1970.

United States Congress Senate Committee on Government Operations. *Organized Crime and Illicit Traffic Narcotics.* Vols. 2–4. Washington, D.C.: Permanent Subcommittee on Investigations, 1963.

United States Federal Narcotics Control Board. *Traffic in Opium and Other Dangerous Drugs.* Washington, D.C.: Bureau of Narcotics, 1957.

Valentine, Douglas. *The Strength of the Wolf: The Secret History of America's War on Drugs.* New York: Verso, 2004.

Varese, Federico. *Mafias on the Move: How Organized Crime Conquers New Territories.* Princeton, NJ: Princeton University Press, 2011.

Vincent, Joseph. *Wise Advice: Touched by the Mafia, Recruited by Law Enforcement.* Gilsum, NH: Pathway Book Service, 2008.

Walker, Stanley. *Dewey: An American of This Century.* Whitefish, MT: Kessinger Publishing, 2005.

Whitehead, Don. *Border Guard: The Story of the United States Customs Service.* New York: McGraw-Hill, 1963.

ABOUT THE AUTHOR

Eric Ferrara is a fourth-generation native New Yorker whose family has lived in Little Italy since the end of the nineteenth century. He is founder and director of the Lower East Side History Project, an award-winning nonprofit research organization; founder of the Museum of the American Gangster in New York City; and a consultant on several television and movie projects worldwide. This is his third title as an author for The History Press.

My great-grandfather Ernest "Cappy" Capitini (not a mobster) in his early century Italian grocery store on Spring Street.